Zodiac of the Gods

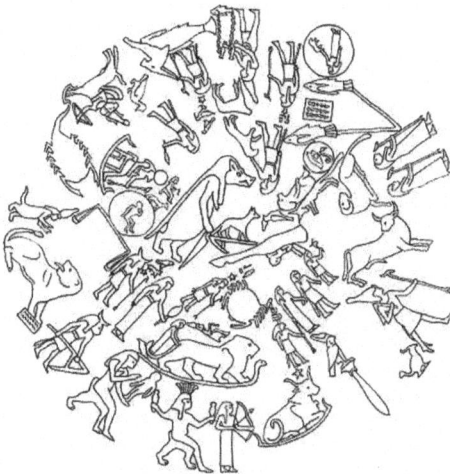

Zodiac of the Gods

A New Interpretation of an Ancient System

Storm Constantine & Graham Phillips

Megalithica Books
Stafford England

Cover Design: Danielle Lainton
Interior Design: Storm Constantine

Set in Palatino Linotype

MB0205

ISBN: 978-1-912241-13-2

A Megalithica Books edition
An imprint of Immanion Press Edition
www.immanion-press.com
info@immanion-press.com

Contents

The Dendera Stela in the Louvre Museum

Introduction

The most familiar natal sign system is that of Western astrology, which takes the patterns and movements of the stars as its basis for determining the characteristics of people born under their influence. The Egyptian-inspired system in this book doesn't involve the stars but rather separate phases within the year. These are of the same number of days as months, but do not follow the pattern of the familiar calendar, roughly the 29th of a month to the 27th of the following month. These periods of time are referred to within this system as phases and follow a version of the Egyptian calendar from a period known as the Late Kingdom, from 664BC to 332BC.

The Ancient Egyptians' interest in astronomy began in prehistoric times. Their lives were ruled by the behaviour of the River Nile, and observations of the celestial bodies in the heavens helped them establish when the annual inundation was likely to occur. The heliacal rising of the star Sopdet (known to us as Sirius and to the Greeks as Sothis) heralded the inundation of the Nile.

The position of the stars and planets had relevance in the religious calendar, in respect of determining the date of festivals. They also were instrumental in the Egyptian understanding of the 'hours of the night', which were connected with the Duat, (the underworld), and the journey of the pharaoh's soul after death. The Duat was divided into twelve hours, each of which was governed by specific gods, goddesses and monsters

Not a great deal remains in terms of documents or stelae to pass on the astrological beliefs of the Egyptians. Star tables have been found painted on the inside of coffins, but the most informative relic is the Dendera Zodiac. This elaborate bas-relief, sculpted on a twelve-inch stone disc, was found on the ceiling of a chapel commemorating the resurrection of Osiris in the Temple of Hathor at Dendera in central Egypt. From this artefact it was discovered that the Ancient Egyptians were aware of five planets in the solar system: Mercury 'the Inert', Venus, 'the god of the morning', Mars, 'Horus the Red', Jupiter 'Horus Who Reveals the Mystery' and Saturn 'Horus the Bull'.

The Dendera stela also shows constellations of the night sky. The stela has been dated to around 50BC, the end of the period known as the New Kingdom. This was the era when the Romans conquered Egypt and began to influence its culture – as well as be influenced in return. The stela is regarded as a comprehensive map of the sky as the Ancient Egyptians saw it, (the only one of its kind), and scholars have suggested that all subsequent astronomical systems derived from it. The stela was removed from the Dendera complex and is now on display in the *Musée de Louvre* in Paris.

The constellations are represented by various animals, and some of them are clearly recognisable as those used in modern astronomy, such as Aries and Capricorn. Others, however, are represented by symbols of relevance particularly to the Egyptians. The zodiac, as far as we know, was never used by the Egyptians for natal analysis. This idea came later, and originated in Greece, which gave rise to our present astrological signs. The signs under which an Egyptian was born were determined by the months of the year. The Dendera zodiac reveals the various gods, goddesses and creatures that presided over each of the months.

This book presents a new interpretation of the Dendera Zodiac. Originally, the information was gathered by lengthy questionnaires sent out to hundreds of volunteers, and the data subsequently analysed in terms of personal characteristics most commonly found in people born in the same months.

However, *Zodiac of the Gods* doesn't focus solely upon character analysis. It also includes magical workings associated with each month and the deity that presided over it. The Ancient Egyptians were immersed in magic – their lives were ruled by rituals and superstitions – and there is no doubt that they revered a plethora of gods and goddesses, whose worship was part of their daily lives; they viewed their host of deities almost as respected companions rather than remote, rarefied figures in some far-off celestial realm.

Throughout Ancient Egyptian history, the year was divided into three seasons of four months, rather than our four seasons of three months. Because of their climate, they did not have a winter as we do. Their seasons were the Inundation, when the River Nile overflowed its banks and fertilised the land with rich, dark soil, the Growing Season, when the people farmed the land, and the Harvest Season, when the crops were gathered in, and the year came to its blistering, parched close before the Inundation began the month again. Each of the twelve months of the year was ruled over by a different god or sacred creature. From inscriptions at the Temple of Hathor, we know that these divinities were thought to influence a person's physical and mental attributes, just as today's zodiac signs are thought to determine personality and appearance. However, to date, no hieroglyphic inscriptions have been found to provide specific details concerning the characteristics of each sign.

At different periods in their history, the Egyptians altered the time of the new year and the start of each month. In the Old Kingdom, (2686-2181 BC), the year began on the Spring Equinox (Mar 21st) The twelve months each ran from the 21st-20th.

The Middle Kingdom began in 2040 BC and lasted until 1782 BC. During this time, the new year coincided with the heliacal rising of the star Sopdet, (Sirius), which occurred in mid-July. The calendar was changed so that the months also began around what is the 15th of the month in our modern calendar. Also, beliefs and systems tended to vary around the country. During the Middle Kingdom, some areas might have retained the original calendar. There were also local variations on the deities associated with each month.

The early calendar followed a lunar month, which meant

that as the years passed, they eventually became slightly out of kilter. To correct this, five extra, or 'epagomenal' days were added to the calendar, which kept the years in alignment. These days fell between what is now 14th –18th July. This is similar to a 'leap year' in our modern calendar, when an extra day is added to February every four years.

The epagomenal days were regarded as sacred and the birthdays of principal gods – the offspring of the god Geb (the earth) and the goddess Nut (the sky). The legends of these deities and the symbols surrounding them are not included specifically in this system, simply because they relate to an earlier calendar than the one used here. However, those who are born on one of these days might find this information interesting, so it's included here simply for information:

14th July	Osiris, Lord of the Underworld, and a god of transition, resurrection and regeneration.
15th July	Horus the Elder, a falcon-headed god (not to be confused with Osiris' own son of the same name, who presides over the months Sept-Oct)
16th July	Set, a god of chaotic forces, disorder, storms and violence.
17th July	Isis, one of the highest goddesses of Ancient Egypt, who was given the epithet 'great in magic'. She became the wife of Osiris.
18th July	Nephthys, a goddess associated with funerary rites. She became the wife of Set, but also had a child with Osiris – the jackal-headed god, Anubis.

By the Late Kingdom, it had become established that the year began with the inundation of the Nile on or around the 29th August. By this time, the calendar had been embellished and more detailed, and it was during this period that the Dendera Zodiac was created. This is the calendar used to create this system.

People have always been fascinated by Ancient Egypt and many feel drawn to its exotic spirituality. The gods themselves, mysterious creatures of sometimes bizarre appearance, inspire the imagination. We can find strength in the image of lioness-headed Sekhmet, lady of power and fire, and a lusty joy for life in the goddess of love, Hathor, who was sometimes depicted as a white cow – although she was mostly represented in art as a beautiful woman. Jackal-headed Anubis is the weigher of hearts, while Ibis-headed Thoth presides over writing and wisdom. Each of the deities who govern the months of the year has particular characteristics and attributes. It could be said they have an 'essence', which flavours the month itself.

The essay at the end of this book, *"Natal Influences on Personality: Science or Superstition?"*, provides an account of the development of astrology and natal signs in general. It explains why recent scientific research suggests that astrology – or any system involving the seasons or lunar months for character analysis – might be somewhat more than superstition or wishful thinking – as detractors tend to regard such systems. There is, in fact, a credible scientific basis as to why such character analysis might be valid.

The first section of the book comprises character and relationships analysis, while the later section focuses upon basic Egyptian magic, including further information about the various gods and goddesses, as well as rituals – or workings – to perform to them.

When you do a magical working, you put your intentions out into the universe, making a connection with the source of all, whether you believe that's a mass of formless energy or a god or goddess. Gods can be seen as masks we put upon the universal life energy, so that we, as humans, can understand it and give it a face. Presented in this book are some of the more exotic faces of this energy, and perhaps in understanding them, you will come to understand more about yourself.

"The Setting of the Sun"
Relief from Temple of Hathor, Dendera

Part One
The Natal Signs

Thoth as a Dog-headed Baboon

Thoth

August 29 – September 27

O great Thoth, lord of the mind and guardian of learning, you are the bringer of knowledge to mankind.

From a first-century papyrus discovered in Alexandria.

The god Thoth is usually depicted with the head of an ibis, although sometimes he was shown having the head of a baboon. He was the lord of the moon, and his name in Ancient Egyptian was Tehuti or Djehuti. He was the lord of time and the god of learning and imagination, presiding over scribes and knowledge, and was himself the scribe of the gods. He was credited with the invention of writing and alphabets – most specifically the Egyptian hieroglyphics. Thoth was often an advisor to the other gods, as his wisdom and judgement were trusted, and he was called upon to arbitrate disputes. While some of his attributes might have varied, according to local tradition, his wife was generally regarded to be Ma'at, a goddess of truth, law, balance and harmony. Seshat, a goddess of wisdom, was either his daughter or, in other versions of his 'history', his wife.

While having many temples throughout Egypt, his main sanctuary was at Khmun, which later became known as Hermopolis Magna, during Roman rule. The Greeks identified him with their god Hermes.

Those born in this sign share an unusual combination of both the materialistic and the imaginative. One of the chief characteristics of the Thoth personality is constantly to question the world about them. They are analytical and self-critical, sometimes to the extent of impeding progress. However, Thoth can achieve remarkable results in a very short time.

In social circumstances, Thoth is often the one to initiate, plan and organise events. However, they can sometimes cause problems for others. Their interests can be so varied that they will change their minds in the middle of a venture or shared project, and those who may have dropped everything to follow them can be left high and dry. This is not because Thoths are insensitive: they naturally assume that others will be like themselves and update their interests if something more appropriate comes along. However, when they are working professionally on behalf of others, Thoth's altruism means that they will see a task through to its conclusion to the very best of their ability.

Although the Thoth type may express a keen interest in the arts, they rarely enjoy concerts or theatre, becoming restless when forced to remain seated for any length of time. Their own interests being original, they enjoy mental rather than physical pastimes. Thoth people seldom join societies, preferring to create their own amusement. Thoths are reluctant leaders, usually preferring to go it alone. Having an abundance of mental energy, they are capable of handling most tasks that befall them. They also have the enviable capacity to land on their feet should a crisis occur.

Positive Qualities

Thoth has great versatility. Endowed with an alert mind and an excellent memory, they are capable of solving many problems that others find difficult. They are especially precise regarding minute detail. Neat and methodical, they take pride in their work. In business, they work best alone, being capable of long periods of focused activity. They are also interested in philosophy and applying it to their lives, and have many original ideas. Thoths also possess an ingrained sense of fairness and justice and will take up the cause of people they believe are being treated unjustly.

Negative Traits

If an enterprise fails, Thoth might become oversensitive and quick to take offence. Pessimism is usual for a Thoth who has suffered a setback. Their typical response to adversity is to withdraw, accepting further problems as if they somehow deserve them. Although critical of themselves, they dislike being criticised by others, and are usually the last people to take advice. Extravagance and impatience can lead to financial problems.

Appearance

Thoth people typically have an upright appearance, with a smooth complexion and warm, attractive eyes. Often large, the eyes are commonly their most striking feature. They tend to be slim with sharp or angular features. Usually they retain a youthful appearance well into middle age. The worry lines that are likely to appear on their faces make them look wiser rather than older.

Health

The parts of the body prone to infection are the stomach and abdomen; indigestion and intestinal difficulties are typical conditions of this sign. They might also suffer from nervous disorders, and some Thoths are prone to hypochondria. Should Thoth research symptoms of illness, they'll think they're coming down with every disease imaginable. Yet they are often the bravest sign when it comes to genuine illness. If they do fall sick or become injured, they cope well and may even continue with their normal routine against medical advice. However, despite their fears, Thoth is a sign of good health and those born in this phase are usually fit and trim.

Optimising Thoth Attributes

Thoth should aim to remain focused on one job at a time, rather than try to juggle numerous tasks simultaneously. Their greatest shortcoming is that they have too many interests, ideas, and skills to devote themselves sufficiently to a single project. Their hypercritical side needs managing, as does their touchiness about being criticised themselves. Extremely sensitive to disapproval, Thoth is often distracted or dissuaded by adverse opinion. They should concentrate more on what they are doing and worry less about what others may think. They should also learn to control the desire to overspend. Although their generosity is admirable, extravagance is always a risk. More than any other sign, money passes quickly through the hands of Thoth.

Suitable Occupations

Writing professions, such as journalism, can be ideal for Thoth, as those born in this sign have inquiring and critical minds. Being natural entertainers, acting or performing of any kind can also be an appropriate career for them. They can also become accomplished musicians. Their outgoing personality and highly-developed social skills means that those born in this sign are ideally suited for careers in sales or public relations. Their eloquence and fair-mindedness, coupled with a flair for the dramatic, makes Thoth an excellent representative for the causes of others and so lawyers, agents and entertainment managers are often born in this sign. As well as being a scribe and a representative of the law, Thoth was also the god of learning, so people born under this sign can be excellent teachers and lecturers, with inventive ways of making their subject matter interesting for students.

The Thoth at Work

Thoths are practical, industrious and conscientious about their work, being particularly methodical in the way they go about it. Walking encyclopaedias, Thoth's hobbies are often related to their jobs. Thoth's inability to relax means that, where possible, they take their work home with them. They have no intention of knocking off the moment the working day ends. Unlike signs who find the thought of after-hours work disagreeable, Thoth usually enjoys it. They work best in short, sharp bursts, however, and dislike being hampered by rules and regulations.

The Thoth Personality

In domestic life, Thoth is neat and tidy, unable to concentrate if surrounded by mess. They prefer to appear well-groomed from the moment their day begins. Their homes will be tastefully furnished and uncluttered, with a preference for light, open and airy rooms. The only untidy place in their home will be the medicine cupboard, which is likely to be crammed with remedies and a well-stocked first aid kit. Thoths tend to be hypochondriacs.

Thoth types are practical and realistic regarding friendships and romantic partnerships. They never expect too much from people and are prepared to work towards a long and happy relationship, with fair give and take. If there is an irresolvable conflict, however, they don't baulk at cutting themselves off and moving on, providing they're sure the situation is really hopeless. Seldom holding grudges, Thoth copes better than others with the breakups of friendships and romantic affairs.

Although they might be somewhat fussy or faddy, Thoths are good socialisers. At ease in all social situations, Thoth has an entertaining sense of humour and a versatile character, making them the heart of any gathering. However, they might sometimes give the impression they're not quite sharing the spirit of the occasion. It's not that they're being rude or disinterested, but rather they might be thinking of more than one thing at once.

If in a relationship, they are prepared to do their fair share of domestic tasks. Thoth takes great care to get to know a prospective partner well before plunging into commitment or marriage. They are generally faithful in relationships, making certain that one has ended before another begins. It's unlikely they'd evade obligations to an ex-partner, or knowingly be responsible for breaking up someone else's relationship.

The Thoth Parent

Thoths make good parents and take a keen interest in their children's education. They bring up their children with concern and kindness, are seldom strict and refrain from any form of punishment unless absolutely necessary. Thoth treats their child as they would an adult, always prepared to explain why something should be done in a particular way. Indeed, Thoths set their children a good example with their tidy habits and considerate manners.

The Thoth Child

Thoths can be difficult children. Although they seldom find themselves in serious trouble, or have a negative attitude to life, the Thoth child can be hyperactive. They rarely sit still and are always inquisitive. They are forever inventing new games to play. They might be the kind of child to break a toy into pieces to modify it for some other purpose. Their creative imagination earns them many friends, but often leads to quarrels with parents or elders. The Thoth child can be extremely tiring.

Thoth children are hardly ever rude and are perhaps the politest young people of any sign. Unfortunately, their sense of humour can get them into trouble, even though their pranks are not deliberately destructive, cruel or malicious. Paradoxically, the same good-humoured jesting by a Thoth adult often results in considerable popularity. At school, the Thoth child may be top of the class, although their restless nature means they are easily distracted. Their teachers might claim they could do much better and should not fool around so much. However, while they may not do so well during term time, when it comes to examinations Thoth invariably makes up for it, being able to catch up with their school-mates through intense revising.

The Thoth Friend

Thoths are generous and entertaining friends. Never short of exciting ideas, they are fun to be with: perhaps the best people with whom to share a night out. They have so many varied interests and experiences, about which they are accomplished story-tellers, that they can keep you engrossed for hours. They have good manners and never cause embarrassment in company.

Sometimes, however, Thoths can be taxing. You may be feeling tired, or in need of peace and quiet, and along comes Thoth with suggestions for activity and adventure. Thoths just can't relax: they have to keep busy and want their friends to be the same.

If you go to them with a problem, Thoths can offer constructive advice, but although they have the best of intentions, there are times when they'll be critical of those close to them. Loyal though they are to their nearest and dearest, they are clear-sighted about the shortcomings of relatives, partners and close friends – and quick to remind them. They often expect too much of others and tend to quibble over minor matters of no real consequence.

Nevertheless, the common good is usually a high priority for Thoth, who is prepared to make personal sacrifices to help those around them.

The Thoth Partner

One of the strangest Thoth traits is their failure to realise when someone they meet (or even already know) is attracted to them. It usually comes as a complete shock when they discover the truth. This is often taken to be a lack of interest on Thoth's part – a common and sometimes unfortunate mistake.

They can be shy when it comes to starting a relationship, which is due to their own self-criticism rather than a lack of confidence. Although they worry too much, and sometimes fail to act, Thoths are generally caring and emotionally uninhibited once they have found the right partner. They have an entertaining personality that heightens their appeal to others. However, they can be so bound up with their careers they are in no hurry to settle down or make commitments.

Relationships are sometimes made difficult by an obstinate spirit. Thoth has a propensity to disregard the attitudes of others or offend without meaning to. They like to consider every angle of a problem, which often leads to too much preparation and not enough action. Frequently, Thoths fail to seize opportunities offered to them on a plate. Once they have found something to which they are committed, however, their devotion is usually total. The accommodating good-nature of a Thoth should not be mistaken as compliance. Those who consider them a pushover are in for a shock.

Thoth and Other Signs

Affinity Signs

ANUBIS AND HATHOR: Thoth particularly enjoys the company of Anubis and Hathor. Hathor's romanticism makes them an eager audience for the imaginative ideas of Thoth. Anubis is also imaginative and together they inspire one another.

THE PHOENIX: Thoth is a mood-swinger and their behaviour can be erratic. Unlike many signs, the Phoenix is almost impervious to the emotional swings of others. As both the Phoenix and Thoth need their own space, they make excellent partners and long-lasting relationships are possible.

THOTH: The Thoth type generally works best with other Thoths. Their mutual creativity helps develop each other's ideas, while two Thoths complement each other in business matters.

Incompatible Signs

OSIRIS AND WADJET: Thoth generally finds the greatest difficulty with Osiris and Wadjet. Both leadership signs, they enjoy taking charge too much for Thoth's liking. Osiris is often too bossy, while Wadjet – in Thoth's opinion – is far too inquisitive.

THE SPHINX: The Sphinx is the sign that Thoth finds hardest to fathom. Their ability to make something out of nothing, and their keen financial sense, are mysteries to Thoth.

AMUN: Amun likes consistency. Thoth enjoys a far too erratic life style for Amun.

Compatibility with Other Signs

HORUS: Although Horus can make a good acquaintance, being inspired by Thoth, they do not necessarily make ideal partners. Thoth lacks the romantic affection that Horus needs.

SEKHMET: Sekhmet's optimism and will to succeed is admired by Thoth, although they may become frustrated by Sekhmet's abrupt changes of plans and failure to see the obvious.

SHU: Thoth is often attracted to the openness of Shu, although Thoth can mentally exhaust Shu who prefers a more serene lifestyle.

ISIS: Although Isis and Thoth mix well socially, relationships or business partnerships can suffer. When together, they tend to behave irresponsibly.

Trends and Influences Through the Year

Over the course of the year Thoth can expect the following influences to affect their lives during the separate Egyptian sign-phases:

THOTH August 29 – September 27:
During their own sign Thoth is at their most self-critical. They may be inclined to concede defeat rather too readily. Relationships and friendships may suffer due to Thoth self-recrimination.

HORUS September 28 – October 27:
The Horus phase, more than any other sign, is a time of new opportunities in romantic or adventurous affairs for Thoth. It is often their most successful period and new opportunities are likely. Thoth people are frequently inspired, and quick to seize the initiative, at this time of year.

WADJET October 28 – November 26:
Wadjet serpent can open many unexpected doors in Thoth's life. Even if problems do occur Thoth is well placed to divert them to their advantage.

SEKHMET November 27 – December 26:
Sekhmet phase is a time of high activity for Thoth. They should be careful not to overwork themselves. Thoth people can become touchy or oversensitive to the opinions of others. They might need to spend time alone during this time.

THE SPHINX December 27 – January 25:
Thoth is generally extravagant by nature. During this phase, they might spend more than they should, or take unnecessary risks. Thoth loves a mystery, and the riddle of the Sphinx may prove disastrous if it is attempted but unsolved. An accepted challenge may well backfire at this time of the year. Thoth should be more cautious than usual during this phase.

SHU January 26 – February 24:
In Egyptian mythology, Shu was a god of good fortune. This is particularly true for Thoth. During this phase, most Thoths find that something long-awaited will finally materialise. Any Thoth seeking fresh romantic attachments may find this time particularly eventful.

ISIS February 25 – March 26:
Isis is specifically a sign of love and romance as far as Thoth is concerned. Successful Thoth relationships are often formed during the phase of Isis.

OSIRIS March 27 – April 25:
Strangely, the phase of Osiris is often a time when Thoth bumps into people they prefer not to meet. It can also be a time of unwelcome news and upset plans. Many Thoths will be happier when the phase of Osiris is complete.

AMUN April 26 – May 25:
During the phase of Amun many Thoth people will be ready for something different in their lives. New opportunities, particularly in social circumstances, are likely. It is also a favourable time for romance.

HATHOR May 26 – June 24:
During the phase of Hathor, Thoth is particularly astute in their approach to their endeavours. It is a time of sound judgement, and many Thoths will benefit from important decisions made during this time. This is their luckiest period for anything involving chance.

THE PHOENIX June 25 – July 24:
Thoth, being a particularly analytical and self-critical sign, can be too cautious during this phase. They might change their minds repeatedly. It is probably the best time of year for them to take a vacation.

ANUBIS July 25 – August 28:
For Thoth, Anubis is the message-bearer and good news is likely. If they are considering a change of home or occupation, now can be a favourable time to start looking.

Horus

September 28 – October 27

*I am the lord of the morning sun. I am one who is with
the sound eye; even when closed I am in its protection.*

From The Egyptian Book of the Dead

The falcon-headed god Horus, (whose name in Ancient
Egyptian was Heru), was the god of the rising sun, and (in one
version of his story) the son of Osiris and Isis. He was a symbol
of divine kingship and risked his very existence to avenge his
father's death and oppose his slayer, Set. During the battle
between the two gods, Horus lost his left eye that, it is said, was
replaced by a precious stone – the ultimate talisman of
protection, resurrection and eternal life. The new eye was
provided by the moon god Khonsu and became known as the
Wadjet or Utchat. It is one of the most well-known and
powerful symbols of the Egyptian belief system.

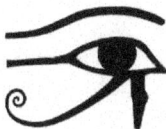

Horus is generally depicted as a man with a falcon's head, wearing a conical crown and a wide pectoral collar. But he could also be represented as a child, known as Horus the Younger, who represented the earliest light of the rising son. In this form he's depicted as a youth, with a lock of hair on the right side of his head, sucking his finger like a young child. There are several versions of Horus in Ancient Egyptian mythology, but this system focuses upon the falcon-headed son of Isis and Osisis. His greatest cult centre was at the Temple of Horus in the city of Edfu, which even to this day remains mostly intact.

Like their mythical counterpart, those born in the sign of Horus often take risks or embark upon enterprises without taking precautions. When the risks pay off, however, enormous success is possible. Horus is stubborn in their convictions, although they make loyal and trustworthy friends. Like the lost talisman, the Eye of Horus, this is a sign of protection, and those born in this phase are usually highly protective of those they love.

Horus loves variety and is always prepared for a new challenge. They have extreme confidence in all endeavours and seldom anticipate disaster or failure. Being so inventive, those born in this sign tend to be absent-minded and are forever losing their personal possessions or mislaying important items. Although at their best during a difficult up-hill struggle, Horus finds it hard to start again if catastrophe should strike.

Essentially good-natured and considerate, Horus is motivated by the urge to get the best from life, whether by adapting themselves to existing conditions or by creating new possibilities. They never attempt to bulldoze their way through obstacles but skilfully navigate their way around them. In Egyptian mythology, Horus was the protector of the animal kingdom and, like their mythical counterpart, many born in this phase have a strong affinity with living creatures of all kinds.

Positive Qualities

Those born in this phase are inventive and creative, having equal artistic and technical flair. Always on the lookout for something new, they are prepared to take risks courageously. Not easily distracted, they have an optimistic attitude towards most of life's demands. They have an emotional and romantic temperament, coupled with a keen interest in the well-being of others. Horus is blessed with an abundance of originality and lets little stand in the way of a fruitful and interesting lifestyle.

Negative Traits

An unrealistic attitude to life can make it difficult for Horus to realise their ambitions. Complications may arise through failure to accept problems or avoid danger. Many born in this sign have a stubborn attitude and can be pig-headed. Horus finds it difficult to accept authority and, especially in their formative years, this can result in conflict with authoritative figures or arguments with parents. Even as a mature adult, this trait persists. Horus does not like being told what to do, even if it's the right thing to do. Most endeavours are all or nothing for Horus and few born in this phase leave anything in reserve.

Appearance

Like the wings of the falcon, the arms are one of the most notable features of Horus. They are long and graceful, and Horus tends to use them expressively in conversation, making wide and exaggerated gestures. Horus people are most at home in casual attire, but their relaxed grace make them look good in anything they wear. Unless it is essential to appear in formal clothes for an occasion, most are content to wear whatever is at hand. When they do dress up, however, Horus usually has an uncommon and individual style of dress.

Health

One problem that many Horus share is insomnia. Few born in

this sign sleep deeply or for long, and restless nights are common. This is especially true if Horus is engaged in a particularly absorbing scheme. Sometimes, stress and prolonged periods of activity can lead to headaches or migraines. The Horus who has suffered a setback often suffers from melancholia or even depression, which is persistent enough to require medical help.

Horus people aren't particularly sporty and many of them loathe exercise, although they might well force themselves to do it for the sake of their health – grudgingly.

Optimising Horus Attributes

Exceptionally creative, Horus's ideas are often unconventional and original, attracting adverse criticism from those who are less imaginative. Few born in this phase will accept censure without a fight. Although others may hold unconventional views in private, Horus says what they feel, and expresses what they believe. This may lead to conflicts that could otherwise have been avoided. Horus should learn to hold their tongue now and again and try a little harder to impress or even flatter those whose help they need. For Horus, what happens today is far more important than what happened yesterday. Horus should avoid burning the bridges they have crossed.

Suitable Occupations

Despite a general antipathy towards sports, a considerable number of successful athletes are born in this phase. This is perhaps because sport requires a person to break through the 'pain barrier' repeatedly or to push themselves beyond endurance; the kind of challenge upon which a Horus thrives.

Horus, in fact, enjoys a degree of personal risk in their undertakings, and not merely physical ones. They can become extremely successful politicians, easily wielding the skills necessary for the role. They have excellent communicative abilities, coupled with an attention-grabbing and persuasive form of expression. Few born in this sign fail to argue their point.

For artistic pursuits, Horus is a particularly creative sign. As managers or employers, however, they are not always the best candidates. Those born in this phase tend to lead far too readily from the front and fail to offer the support and encouragement others may need.

The Horus at Work

As a negotiator, the persistent Horus excels. Bargaining can be a long and arduous affair, and Horus is an able player at the waiting game. Those who believe that they are getting the better of any deal with Horus are deluding themselves. Horus will go to any lengths to achieve their aims. Many born in this phase are self-made people, having a style all their own. However, headstrong emotions can send them forging ahead, and others may find it difficult to keep pace. Many Horus people have an eccentric personality that workmates will either love or hate. Horus makes an excellent ally but a formidable opponent.

The Horus Personality

To those born in this sign, what they are doing is far more important than how they look. While Horus is prepared to dress smartly to suit an occasion or to conform at work, they are generally more comfortable in informal, comfortable attire that allows them to project an aura of relaxed confidence while not feeling constricted.

Horus can be the toughest of any sign. They are good socialisers and are usually popular with others – over whom they can exert much influence. Shyer or more reserved people might find Horus somewhat daunting, as they control the people in their life with ease. It's unlikely someone born in this phase would be attracted to a domineering partner. Horus picks out the partner they want and pursues them with determination.

Horus types are imaginative, witty and erudite. However, they aren't everyone's idea of the perfect date. They might be marvellous company, full of anecdotes, jokes and fun, but occasionally can have an unusual, sometimes eccentric manner that can be intimidating. Moreover, Horus says exactly what they think, which may not always be what their partner wants to hear. Luckily, Horus prefers partners with an unconventional attitude to life – few others can take them in their stride.

Horus is adventurous and always ready to lead. However, they seem unaware that others may have difficulty keeping pace. One trait that might manifest is a propensity for gambling, of being unable to resist the temptation of trying to make money the effortless way. It's common for Horus to be inept at managing their own finances. The most extreme examples despise the idea of thrift. They are often late paying their bills and all too willing to obtain credit they can't afford to repay. However, Horus is luckier than many signs – their excesses often pay off.

The Horus Parent

Horus is an affectionate and protective parent though not usually possessive. Their children are encouraged to be self-reliant and to mix freely with others. Horus parents like to be considered as friends to their children rather than disciplinarians, and many Horus offspring maintain this easy relationship with their parents throughout their lives. Horus parents never suffer from the frequent problem of expecting too much of their young. They may have unrealistic ambitions for themselves, but such harsh expectations are seldom inflicted on others.

The Horus Child

Horus children are the most contrary of any sign. From an early age, they are forever disagreeing with teachers or parents. It is no good merely telling a Horus child that something simply *is* – you will always be faced with an abrupt 'Why?' Many Horus children are overly energetic which, coupled with their natural inquisitiveness, can make them something of a handful. The questioning Horus is quick to learn, however, and providing their curiosity is accommodated they can be as entertaining as their adult counterparts.

Most children are untidy, but Horus especially so. On the positive side, they are generally concerned about the well-being of others, and few Horus children will be cruel or unkind. In fact, they have a sympathetic attitude to others right from infancy and are sometimes far too ready to aid. When in trouble, children tend to deny responsibility and accuse a friend or sibling. The Horus child, however, is usually willing to admit fault and may even take the blame on behalf of their friends.

The Horus Friend

Horus is tremendous fun to have around. They share a marvellous, although unusual, sense of humour, live life to the full and can be the soul of any gathering. They have an abundance of energy, love being the centre of attention, and have a great aptitude to think up novel and interesting schemes. However, Horus can be somewhat draining – they never seem to stop. For some signs, Horus is best in small doses. Others who enjoy the unusual are often at their happiest in the company of the exciting Horus. But beware! Horus also expects to share their problems. With most born in this sign, friendship is an all-or-nothing affair.

Horus is quick to forgive and seldom holds a grudge – unless, that is, someone has deliberately done them harm. When Horus has what they believe to be a justifiable grievance they are expert at exacting revenge. They can stir up trouble for their enemies by skilfully setting others at their throats, while all the time remaining apparently blameless.

Horus may have much to say, but they often have little patience with mulling over old hurts or painfully analysing the past. Primarily, they live for today and tomorrow.

The Horus Partner

Horus is not inclined to feign an interest in matters that fail to absorb them. If they are bored, they will say so. This can sometimes lead to conflicting behaviour in the caring Horus. If impelled by circumstances to be involved in something in which they have no real interest, they consider it a tiresome, duty-bound responsibility. Consequently, they will carry out what is expected of them but make certain that everyone knows exactly how they feel. It is often advisable for a partner to exclude Horus from anything in which they have no enthusiasm. Horus will quite happily apply themselves to something else.

Horus is a complainer, especially about the service in hotels, restaurants or stores. Occasionally, especially during journeys and vacations, Horus's grouching and moaning can be painful. It is usually best for Horus's partner to handle receptionists, waiters and other serving staff – it will certainly make life easier for everyone concerned.

Horus may not be the most romantic of partners for a date, but they desperately need love in their lives. Born in a particularly caring sign, they have a deeply sentimental streak; they need and offer true affection. They may say exactly what they feel, they may be inclined to moan, but Horus can fall madly in love and will make personal sacrifices to assure their partner's happiness. Those born in the sign of Horus might be individuals, but they are certainly not loners.

Horus and Other Signs

Affinity Signs

OSIRIS: Both signs are particularly tolerant of one another. Horus's shortcomings are like Osiris's own, such as escaping wherever possible from tiresome responsibilities. Both hate to be tied down. With so many interests, Horus seldom finds themselves in conflict with Osiris.

WADJET: Although Wadjet and Horus are opposites in many respects, their traits and attributes are complimentary. Wadjet is patient and plans long and hard; Horus can be impatient and impetuous. The serpent can restrain the hawk, while Horus can bring more spontaneity to Wadjet's life.

THE SPHINX: Horus and the Sphinx often mix well. The Sphinx has many ideas that they lack the courage to try. Horus is quite prepared to implement the Sphinx's schemes. These signs often make ideal partners.

Incompatible Signs

THE PHOENIX: Potentially the most problematic combination for Horus. The Phoenix recovers well from failure and setback, but Horus finds it hard. Both signs are adventurous but – in legend – when the Phoenix burned it rose again. The two signs get on great to begin with, but should problems occur the Phoenix cannot understand Horus's inability to cope.

SEKHMET: Energetic Sekhmet and stubborn Horus will often argue and bicker even when they see eye-to-eye.

SHU: The serene lifestyle Shu needs is unlikely to be found with Horus.

Compatibility with Other Signs

THOTH: Although Thoth can become good friends with Horus, they do not necessarily make ideal romantic partners. Thoth lacks the romantic affection that Horus needs.

AMUN: Horus is a particularly affectionate sign, and Amun tends to distrust open displays of affection. Amun, however, can sometimes provide an emotional balance for Horus.

HATHOR: Horus and Hathor both allow their imaginations free reign. Consequently, the two signs get on well but may behave irresponsibly when together.

ANUBIS: Anubis and Horus have few problems socially, although Horus is seldom prepared to make the sort of long-term commitments Anubis expects.

HORUS: Together, those born in this sign tend to behave in a completely impractical manner and financial considerations are usually ignored. In social circumstances, however, they are usually fascinated by each other's attitude to life and deeply enjoy each other's company.

ISIS: As both Horus and Isis commit themselves so completely to a chosen pursuit, these two signs work well together if they share a similar heart-felt interest. If their interests lie in different directions, however, they are unlikely to have the time to spare for one another.

Trends and Influences Through the Year

Over the course of the year Horus can expect the following influences to affect their lives during the separate Egyptian sign-phases:

THOTH August 29 – September 27:
Thoth is the message-bearer for Horus. During this phase Horus can expect favourable news.

HORUS September 28 – October 27:
During their own phase, Horus can be especially reckless. They should think long and deeply about any change of direction they may be considering. If an enterprise has been long-established, however, a favourable turn of events is likely - if Horus lets things be as they are.

WADJET October 28 – November 26:
The serpent brings Horus a period of much success in social and leisure activities. Sporting events are particularly favoured at this time. Indeed, games of any kind can be enjoyed to the full, often with remarkable success. A lucky period for ventures involving risk.

SEKHMET November 27 – December 26:
Anything concerning group activities, either social or business in nature, is well placed for Horus. Any Horus who takes the initiative at this time of year is likely to find themselves in a profitable position. This may be the most romantic period of the year for those born in the sign of Horus.

THE SPHINX December 27 – January 25:
The Sphinx's guardian role is influential over Horus during this phase, but in a restrictive sense. Nearly everything Horus tries to accomplish seems to be prevented and all that they hope for delayed.

SHU January 26 – February 24:
During the phase of Shu, Horus's plans may prove impractical. They may find themselves out of touch with everyday events and relationships, or social events may suffer from Horus's unrealistic expectations.

ISIS February 25 – March 26:
Isis is a sign of change for Horus. Horus may feel the urge to change job, social or even romantic attachments at this time. Exciting and promising opportunities are also on the cards. This is a particularly propitious time for Horus people considering a change of any kind.

OSIRIS March 27 – April 25:
Osiris has a positive effect on Horus. Many of their imaginative enterprises will come to fruition. New relationships or business links formed at this time may prove positive for Horus. Love, romance and affairs of the heart are particularly well-favoured during this phase.

AMUN April 26 – May 25:
During this phase, Horus is often at their most adventurous. Their fun-loving disposition is best directed toward leisure activities, and many will find a vacation exhilarating. Any Horus on the lookout for new romantic attachments may be pleasantly surprised during this period.

HATHOR May 26 – June 24:
The phase of Hathor is when Horus is likely to make errors of judgement. When the headstrong influences of Hathor and Horus combine, it can result in a lack of tact or restraint.

THE PHOENIX June 25 – July 24:
The resourceful Phoenix brings many new opportunities for Horus. At no other time of the year is Horus so ready to succeed, especially in commercial ventures.

ANUBIS July 25 – August 28:
This phase is not a good one for Horus to make any important decisions or major changes in lifestyle. It is best to wait for the time of Anubis to pass before doing anything likely to cause long-term effects.

Amulet Depicting Wadjet with the Body of a Winged Serpent

Wadjet

October 28 – November 26

*It is through the will of the great serpent goddess
that all kings shall rule.*

From the Pyramid Texts

Wadjet, known also as Uatchat, was the royal cobra goddess of Ancient Egypt. (There is also a connection, as can be seen by her name, with the Eye of Horus, also known as the Wadjet.) She was believed to have created the papyrus swamps of the Delta. One of her epithets was 'the Green One', referring to this function. She was often depicted as having green skin. As a deity of kingship, her image as a serpent adorned the front of the pharaoh's crown, when it was called the Uraeus. She was generally depicted as a cobra poised to strike. Originally, she was the patron goddess of a city named Dep, which later became known as Per-Wadjet, and was then renamed by the Greeks as Buto. Its modern name is Desouk.

Wadjet is typically represented in art as a cobra-headed woman, or simply as a cobra wearing a crown, and sometimes having wings. She was also occasionally depicted as a woman with two serpent heads, or a serpent with the head of a woman. Occasionally, in her role as an Eye of Ra, (like Sekhmet), she was shown with a lioness's head.

Wadjet was a symbol of knowledge and those born in this sign often exude an aura of wisdom. Wadjet people have logical and calculating minds. They are adept at formulating plans and waiting patiently for the precise moment to act. Although they enjoy the virtue of patience, they live constantly in a state of readiness. Like the snake, they strike instantly when the time is right. Wadjets are dedicated and conscientious workers. They are eager to learn and quick to find practical applications for their knowledge. Often, it is Wadjet who is called upon to deal with problems others have failed to solve.

Wadjets are prepared to work long and hard to achieve their objectives. They are highly ambitious, seldom deterred by adversity and almost oblivious to hostile opinion. Although Wadjets share a pragmatic and materialistic attitude to life, they approach nothing in a dull or tedious fashion. Indeed, most Wadjets ooze enthusiasm for their chosen subjects. They may be given to high-spirited and frivolous behaviour in their spare time, but during working hours they are serious and determined. Wadjets are realists, directing their energy toward their endeavours with logic and common sense, rather than what they would consider lofty intuition.

Wadjets have immense patience and accurately judge the correct moment to act in any situation. They also have the capacity to grasp the root of a problem, possessing shrewd insight into the real cause of difficulties they may face. In any enterprise, Wadjet will weigh up its potential long and hard before making decisions. Wadjets are forthright and astute. They have inquiring and probing minds and are remarkably self-disciplined.

Positive Qualities

Wadjets have a serious outlook on life, coupled with an intense sense of responsibility. Their ambition is supported by a shrewd intellect and the ability to devote themselves exclusively to whatever tasks they undertake. Observant and inquisitive, Wadjet is quick to learn. They are especially loyal to their friends and take family values seriously. Mental energy is a marked feature of those born in this sign, together with a direct and decisive manner. Many Wadjets show considerable initiative in the handling of financial affairs.

Negative Traits

A cynical temperament may restrict social activities. Often too ready to disregard the opinions of others, arrogance is sometimes a Wadjet fault. Occasionally, Wadjets have an unsympathetic attitude to others. They also tend to take themselves much too seriously at times.

Wadjet is economically-minded and may be over-thrifty, even miserly. Feeling themselves set firmly in the material world, Wadjets often lack spirituality of any kind and tend to despise it in others as superstitious nonsense. This lack of an inner life can lead to arrogant aloofness. And yet, strangely, Wadjet has extraordinary intuition, which they most likely put down to a scientific mode of thinking. To Wadjet, acting on a hunch does not involve risk-taking.

Appearance

Like the head of a swaying cobra, Wadjets will use their hands as a prominent means of expression. If they disagree, they will slice their hands through the air as if to cut the conversation dead, and when they have had enough they will thrust out their palms to call for silence. Some snakes are said to mesmerise their prey. Naturally graceful, many Wadjets have melodic voices possessing an almost hypnotic quality.

Health

Wadjet is especially susceptible to coughs and colds. If a flu virus is going around, Wadjet is sure to catch it. Cold, damp weather also plays havoc with those born in this sign. They thrive in the hottest of climates, but if it is chilly or wet the Wadjet is likely to suffer. Rheumatism, arthritis and similar complaints may be a problem for Wadjets, especially in later years.

Optimising Wadjet Attributes

Wadjets can be far too cynical at times, refusing to believe anything that has not been proved beyond reasonable doubt. They are unlikely to take anything at face value, or on someone else's word. Wadjets should try to have a little more faith in human nature. This might not be a perfect world, but others are generally more honest than Wadjet is prepared to believe. Another Wadjet trait is the need to know the detailed affairs of those around them. Sometimes Wadjets are just too inquisitive for their own good. Few Wadjets will reveal their own motivations, feelings and intentions, however. Those born in this sign would make excellent poker players, if they were inclined to gamble. To Wadjets, however, anything based chiefly upon luck is strictly a mug's game. Wadjet would benefit from taking an occasional risk in life. Too much caution can hold them back.

Suitable Occupations

Wadjets make good entrepreneurs, managers or supervisors. They watch and listen carefully before arriving at conclusions, and then only after every angle has been considered. Accordingly, they make solid judgements and usually take sound commercial decisions. Furthermore, they are quick to assert authority in a firm, decisive manner. Occupations involving intricate, detailed or complex calculations are ideal for Wadjets. They work well with figures and excel in financial careers. Architects, designers and engineers also include many successful Wadjets. Their keen eye for detail makes them ideal for work involving proofreading, editing or copywriting. Wadjets are also suited to academic and teaching occupations and anything involving investigation or research.

The Wadjet at Work

Wadjets apply themselves with remarkable dedication. They have the enviable ability to concentrate fully on whatever they are doing. Employers can always rely on Wadjet to do their job to the best of their ability. Snakes are solitary hunters and the same goes for many born in this phase. They sometimes find it difficult to socialise with colleagues, often preferring to keep their work mates quite separate from their social lives.

The Wadjet Personality

Whatever Wadjet puts their mind to they carry out in a responsible and determined manner. They might be dedicated to their career, but family always comes first. Wadjet prefers to devote themselves exclusively to whatever they are doing, whether as a career person or a home-maker.

Wadjet is a creature of thrift and economy. They take pride in their appearance, but are unlikely to spend a lot of money buying expensive clothes just for the sake of it. Instead, they are more likely to spend their time and money keeping themselves fit and healthy. However, should their work necessitate maintaining a particular image, Wadjet will go to considerable lengths to make certain they fulfil that requirement – simply because it is part of their work. Wadjets can be ideal candidates for a career spent in the public eye or before the camera.

Wadjets consider physical fitness very important. They may be regular visitors to the gym, swimming baths or squash court but are unlikely to be ardent supporters or spectators of sports. Many Wadjets are more concerned with business affairs than leisure-time activities. To them, keeping fit is a physical necessity, like eating or sleeping.

Wadjets have a practical attitude towards life, tackling obstacles and setbacks with logical thinking. They can be helpful advisors for friends and colleagues, through their ability to give sound, objective analysis of any problem. They are also proficient at coming up with solutions. Wadjet is a shrewd investor, well-versed in the unwritten rules of the business world.

Wadjet is a sociable creature but refuses to involve themselves in irrelevant small talk. They are sparing with their affections; others usually need to share their sentiments before Wadjet is prepared to commit themselves to friendship. With friends and loved ones, Wadjet is a constant source of fascinating information. Not only will they know their pet interests inside out, they will air their opinions in an engaging and interesting manner.

The Wadjet Parent

Wadjets make responsible parents, devoting much time and effort to secure their children's future. They are exceptionally keen to see their offspring do well at school or in college. The child of a Wadjet parent is often an academic achiever. They enjoy considerable parental support and encouragement from an early age. Wadjet parents are more likely than others to teach their children to read and write before they go to school. Older children will benefit from their parents' help with their homework. Wadjet parents spare no expense in providing their children with books, learning aids and educational toys. They are happy to spend their money to ensure that their children get the very best start in life.

The Wadjet Child

Wadjets are studious children. They often devote more time to learning than they do to play. Sometimes they may even need encouragement to mix with other children. Many Wadjet children prefer adult company. They mature early and can stand their ground in most situations. Keen observation and intelligence combined with well-developed intuition, often results in 'an old head on young shoulders'.

Wadjet children constantly question the world about them, not satisfied until they have discovered the answer for everything that grabs their attention.

Unlike many young people, the Wadjet child is particularly good with finances. Pocket money is unlikely to be blown at the first opportunity on trivial treats and toys; instead, it's saved towards something more important and lasting. Like their adult counterparts, the Wadjet child is seldom wasteful and has a thrifty attitude toward life in general.

The Wadjet Friend

Although Wadjet is a sign of confidence, many born in this phase are wary of casual acquaintances. Wadjet is cautious by nature, and others may need to prove themselves worthy of their trust. Wadjets expect much in return for their friendship, and in this respect aren't tolerant of the vagaries of human nature. They expect to share and share alike with their friends, and hate to feel excluded from any area of their lives. To a Wadjet, once their friendship has been given, it's a precious thing to be treated with respect. Should a friend compromise this by acting or speaking carelessly, or not keeping Wadjet's feelings forefront in their mind, Wadjet may consider the friendship broken.

Although Wadjets are dedicated workers they also know how to have a good time. They can devote themselves as much to entertainment as they do to work – an evening out is expected to be a fun-filled excursion. During social occasions, the one thing Wadjet cannot abide is someone talking shop. Those who continue a workplace conversation, or even bring up the subject of work, are likely to find themselves immediately cut short by an irritated Wadjet.

Although Wadjets will readily enjoy themselves, they do not seek to be the centre of attention in their social circle. Wadjets may be self-assured but they are also self-conscious, even if they keep this hidden. Few Wadjets are prepared to make a fool of themselves on the dance floor, or to get drunk and lose control.

The Wadjet Partner

Wadjets are seldom eager to show their feelings. They need to trust someone completely before sharing their true emotions. Consequently, the Wadjet partner may need to make all the first moves. Although witty in conversation, Wadjets are frequently shy with potential partners, finding it difficult to initiate a conversation with someone they find attractive. Often, someone will fail to realise that a Wadjet is interested in them romantically.

Wadjets are sensitive and committed lovers but break-ups are particularly difficult for them to handle. They hate the thought that they may have given so much of themselves only to be rejected. On the outside, they seem to cope, but inside they may be devastated, with long-lasting consequences, which they do not talk about. A failed relationship can create an especially cynical Wadjet. Few Wadjets continue to chase or seek the attentions of an ex-partner; they have too much pride. This might give rise to problems in their next relationship. They might be suspicious of the true intentions of their future partner or restrained in the commitments they themselves are prepared to make. It can be some time before Wadjet has recovered sufficiently from a breakup to again abandon their emotional inhibitions.

Wadjet and Other Signs

Affinity Signs

AMUN: Wadjet is a sign of wisdom and those born in this phase are particularly creative concerning practical endeavours. Amun is a materialist and so the two signs complement one another. Both signs lead similar social lives and close friendships and attachments are common.

HORUS: Although Wadjet and Horus are opposites in many respects, their traits and attributes are complimentary. Wadjet is patient and plans long and hard; Horus can be impatient and impetuous. The wise serpent can restrain the impetuous hawk, while Horus can bring more spontaneity to Wadjet's life.

THE SHPINX: The wise Wadjet and the cunning Sphinx usually share a common outlook on life and enjoy many of the same interests. Mutual respect, affection and compatibility are often found between people of these signs.

ISIS: Wadjet love of learning is much respected by Isis. Wadjet finds Isis's unique insight equally fascinating. The two signs work well together, and partnerships are often successful.

Incompatible Signs

THOTH: Wadjet is generally the sign with which Thoth finds greatest difficulty. Wadjets enjoy taking charge too much for Thoth's liking.

THE PHOENIX: Phoenix people find it difficult to cope with the leadership qualities of Wadjet. Wadjets sometimes find Phoenixes too inconsistent in their behaviour.

WADJET: As many Wadjets are somewhat reserved by nature, and unwilling to reveal their inner feelings, two Wadjets together tend to be overcautious in their attitudes to one another.

Compatibility with Other Signs

OSIRIS: Wadjet and Osiris mix well enough, although close relationships are rare. Wadjets are too pragmatic and take life too seriously for Osiris. Many Wadjets consider Osiris to be irresponsible.

HATHOR: Hathor finds the learned Wadjet of considerable interest. They may, however, distrust Wadjet's cool, laid-back approach to life.

SHU: Shus and Wadjets have little in common. However, this can sometimes lead to successful partnerships. There is little for them to argue or disagree about.

ANUBIS: Anubis likes to know precisely where they stand with others and most find Wadjet difficult to fathom.

SEKHMET: Many Wadjets feel that Sekhmets reveal too much about themselves and some may regard this as a weakness. Sekhmets, for their part, may consider that Wadjets lead a far too conventional lifestyle.

Trends and Influences Through the Year

Over the course of the year Wadjet can expect the following influences to affect their lives during the separate Egyptian sign-phases:

THOTH August 29 – September 27:
The phase of Thoth can be full of surprises for Wadjet. This is also an excellent time for a vacation.

HORUS September 28 – October 27:
Horus acts as the message-bearer for Wadjet. Wadjets can expect favourable news during this phase.

WADJET October 28 – November 26:
Wadjets work remarkably well during their own phase. For those involved in academic pursuits, this is a period of much

reward. Wadjets in business also fare particularly well at this time. In domestic matters, positive news concerning financial affairs can be expected.

SEKHMET November 27 – December 26:
There could be conflicts of interest during this phase. Particularly in relationships, Wadjet should avoid disputes. The working Wadjet should also be careful of disagreements in the workplace; things may not work out the way they intended.

THE SPHINX December 27 – January 25:
Wadjet has little difficulty solving the Sphinx's eternal riddle. A long-standing enterprise may come to fruition. This is a time especially favourable for new relationships, romance and love. It is also a lucky period for anything connected with chance.

SHU January 26 – February 24:
Shu is light and air, while the serpent lives its life on the ground. The two signs accordingly have little influence upon one another. This can be a time of inactivity, even boredom, for Wadjet.

ISIS February 25 – March 26:
The phase of Isis can bring a Wadjet plan to fruition. It is also the time of year when new opportunities arise. It is an especially good period for a change of job or home, should either be sought.

OSIRIS March 27 – April 25:
Osiris is a positive sign for Wadjet. This is a favourable time for relationships to flourish. Success is especially likely for Wadjet on the lookout for a new partner.

AMUN April 26 – May 25:
Wadjets are inquisitive and like to know exactly what is going

on around them. Amun can cloud Wadjet's vision – there may be too much happening for Wadjets to see in all directions. They should avoid being suspicious of situations of which they are not fully informed.

HATHOR May 26 – June 24:
Wadjet is a creature of the earth and so is Hathor. The two signs work well together, and Wadjet will find that others will see things their way. This is a particularly favourable phase for sport and leisure activities. Any Wadjet involved in competition is likely to be rewarded with much success.

THE PHOENIX June 25 – July 24:
The usual success of Wadjet's serpent-quick response can be upset during the phase of the Phoenix. In legend, the Phoenix burned to ashes and so opportunities can go up in smoke for a Wadjet during this period.

ANUBIS July 25 – August 28:
In the phase of Anubis financial matters and business affairs are well placed. This is also a romantic time for Wadjet.

Sekhmet

O mighty one, great of magic,
wise and powerful daughter of Ra.

An eighteenth-dynasty inscription
from the temple of Mut

The lioness-headed Sekhmet was both a war and a desert goddess. She was also a mistress of fire and known as the 'Eye of Ra', exemplifying the intense heat of the sun. Her name means 'The Powerful One'. She was always depicted as a lioness-headed woman, and in colour representations was dressed in red. One of her epithets is 'Lady of the Bright Red Linen', which some say refers to blood and her blood-thirsty nature.

Fire-breathing Sekhmet was perhaps the most feared of all Egyptian gods, yet she was also seen as a deity of mystical power, and paradoxically, a goddess of healing. Sekhmet's priests were also physicians. She was considered responsible for the diseases that broke out during the dry season, when the Nile shrank and insects multiplied, and it was considered that as she was proficient at inflicting disease she must also know the best way to cure it. Generally, though, she was a goddess of the pharaoh rather than ordinary people, being petitioned to smite enemies of the country. A shrine to Sekhmet still remains in the temple complex of Karnak, which contains a well-preserved statue of the goddess.

Reflecting the traits of the fierce and protective lioness, those born in the sign of Sekhmet often find that others will feel vulnerable or threatened in their presence. Despite this, many seek the guidance and leadership of Sekhmets, because their power feels protective. Sekhmets, however, are reluctant leaders, usually preferring to go it alone. Blessed with an abundance of mental energy, they are capable of handling most tasks that come to them. Natural creatures of fire, Sekhmets have the enviable capacity not to get burned by circumstances, and – like a cat – usually land firmly on their feet.

Sekhmets possess intellectual vitality, mental dexterity and a lively imagination. Sekhmet is one of the most eloquent of signs and many Sekhmets can argue with an opponent until the other is drained of words. Those born in this phase have endless optimism for their chosen pursuits. Forever formulating plans and innovative ideas, Sekhmets can sometimes be tiring, even exhausting, for friends and acquaintances. Not only are Sekhmets blessed with boundless faith and optimism, they are also endowed with vision and foresight. They have a deep sense of intuition and seem to know precisely what others are thinking and planning. An alert mind enables Sekhmets to determine the full potential of opportunities and make quick decisions. Sekhmets are highly active and many born in this sign excel in sport and games.

Sekhmets work remarkably well in short, sharp bursts. They

apply themselves with speed and determination to whatever they are doing. They have a multiplicity of talents, both creative and practical. With an astute memory and an inquiring mind, those born in this sign are especially clever at arguing a point. They can skilfully side-track an opponent and tie opponents up with their own words. Many Sekhmets are highly intelligent and able to grasp the most complex of problems. They excel at solving conundrums or riddles of any kind. Sekhmets are exceptionally optimistic and refuse to concede defeat under any circumstances. They make quick decisions and act decisively.

Positive Qualities

An energetic personality guarantees Sekhmet success in most undertakings. Extremely versatile, they can turn their hands to all kinds of tasks. Mentally agile and quick to learn, the majority of those born in this sign are observant and possess a remarkably good memory. They have artistic talents, especially in writing and music, and express themselves in a popular, dramatic fashion. With an exceptional ability to cope in times of difficulty, Sekhmets are optimistic and enthusiastic about whatever they are doing.

Negative Traits

Sekhmets are unwilling to change their opinions, even when proved wrong. They are impatient, jump to conclusions far too quickly and are apt to make errors of judgement based on hasty decisions or first impressions. Many born in this sign have a quarrelsome temperament, often disagreeing for the sheer sake of it – and also because they love a good argument! Impulsiveness sometimes stems from their love of action, and they tend to rush headlong into ventures much too readily.

Appearance

Sekhmets are energetic and restless, finding it difficult to sit quietly for any length of time. They need to keep occupied, many being slim or even skinny as a consequence of the nervous energy they expend. Many born in this sign have expressive faces with a rigidly-defined bone structure and penetrating eyes.

Health

Sekhmets are remarkably resilient to viral infections, usually immune to the coughs and colds to which others annually succumb. They seldom get headaches, stomach bugs or any such common complaints. When Sekhmet does fall ill – which is rarely – it is generally with something unusual. The only drawback to Sekhmet's robust constitution is their need for sleep. Deprived of their eight or more hours, Sekhmets will virtually cease to function. At best, the tired Sekhmet will be irritable, grumpy and unable to concentrate.

Optimising Sekhmet Attributes

Sekhmet possesses an abundance of positive traits, but in excess they can evolve into negative traits. Sekhmets can optimise the positive by being self-aware, and not allowing their enthusiasms and stubbornness to sabotage their plans. Their optimistic streak is a considerable drawback if something is an obvious failure. Their stubborn refusal to concede defeat will sometimes tie Sekhmets to a doomed endeavour, preventing them from applying themselves to anything fresh. Their displays of boundless enthusiasm can also be misleading to others. Acquaintances may be captivated by a Sekhmet's idea, only to discover that their interest was only superficial. Sekhmets should work towards moderating their behaviour. It is not that they are deceitful – they simply have tunnel vision.

Suitable Occupations

Sekhmets are suited for occupations involving quick reactions or calculations. They also excel in work that necessitates close customer contact, such as sales. They have a lively personality with a friendly and enthusiastic expression. Many lecturers and teachers are born in this sign, as are writers and broadcasters. Journalism and other investigative work also have strong appeal to Sekhmets. Their mental dexterity, often coupled with a devotion to physical fitness, means that many professional athletes and successful sportspeople are born in this sign.

The Sekhmet at Work

Sekhmets value their freedom above all else. They hate being restricted or compromised in any situation. For this reason, they are best suited to occupations that allow them freedom of movement and the scope to make decisions and handle matters in their own fashion. Sekhmets aim to reach the very pinnacle of whatever profession they choose. Even when not in a position of power they need the authority to use their own initiative. They are generally popular with colleagues, although they may sometimes disturb those with whom they work closely. Sekhmets tend to adopt a loud or flamboyant working style.

The Sekhmet Personality

Sekhmets have an aura of self-confidence and a glowing personality. While some of the more aloof lions might keep their fiery temperament hidden beneath a cool exterior, most Sekhmets tend to display their vitality to full advantage and can captivate an audience effortlessly on social occasions. They can hold their ground, whatever situation they find themselves in, able to improvise proficiently so as not to lose face.

Many people born in this sign are keen on physical fitness. Sekhmet is most comfortable in casual clothes during their leisure times, even if they can conjure an image of power and confidence in the way they dress at work. However, although they can appear groomed, if not polished, they're not overly concerned about domestic tidiness. A great lover of animals, it's not unusual for a Sekhmet to own many pets. Even if their circumstances only permit a single cat or dog, it will be treated as one of the family.

Sekhmets ooze power and confidence and are adept at concealing frailty or insecurity. Such feelings would irritate them immensely.

Many Sekhmets seem to be born performers. Not only are they excellent entertainers, at ease in most circumstances, they can adapt their style and humour to suit any occasion. Sekhmets love to fill their life with excitement, even mystery. Unlike some signs who might find it necessary to create an enigmatic aura to hide a lack of self-confidence, Sekhmet just loves to fascinate those around them. They are children at heart, always eager to be the centre of attention and the lively soul of any gathering.

Most Sekhmets are attracted to dominant partners, admiring strength and power in others. In their home lives, they can be the laziest and most untidy of people, and are most content when whoever shares their home is prepared to organise this side of their life.

The Sekhmet Parent

Sekhmets encourage their children to do well, although they will seldom push them too hard. They usually manage to inspire their children through sheer enthusiasm. Sekhmets have the marvellous ability to make life interesting, and learning can be a fascinating and exciting experience for children of a Sekhmet parent. They are always ready to take time from whatever they are doing – no matter how important – to help and advise their young. Sekhmets run a happy but not a particularly tidy home. They are ready to go to any lengths to prepare their children for working life, but neatness and orderly habits are something their offspring will need to learn elsewhere.

The Sekhmet Child

Sekhmet children demand much attention and need many outlets for their energy. They mix well with others, young and old alike, but tend to monopolise everyone in their vicinity. They may be gifted artistically, academically or technically, but the ability to apply themselves to school or college work is often lacking. They are just too easily distracted. Their intelligence and capacity to rapidly assimilate information provides many born in this sign with the potential to be top of the class – if only they concentrate a little more.

The young Sekhmet may lack concentration in school, gazing through the classroom window at something more exciting outside. When they apply themselves, however, they are immensely creative achievers. Although they may become good sportspeople in their mid-teens, sporting events are not high on the list of the younger Sekhmet's priorities. The Sekhmet child prefers to perform alone rather than as part of an organised group or team.

The Sekhmet Friend

Sekhmets have a wonderful sense of humour, although in some this can veer into being zany. They always have the right joke or pertinent remark for any occasion. They are hospitable and friendly, warm with their friends, and generous natured. Sekhmets need to be constantly occupied and their friends will seldom be bored in their company.

Sekhmets are not particularly keen on the more conservative forms of entertainment. Sitting quietly at the theatre or cinema, or just relaxing in front of the television, is unlikely to appeal to the majority of Sekhmets. They prefer to be actively entertained, if not personally involved. Sekhmets intend to live life to the full and usually expect others to do likewise. If a friend prefers a more serene lifestyle, they are unlikely to get much peace with Sekhmet around. Sekhmets like to keep in touch with distant friends, but their circle of acquaintances is often so large that it may be some time before they finally get around to contacting each in turn.

One annoying habit that is almost Sekhmet's trademark is the tendency for them to take far too long to get ready to go out. 'I'll just be a minute,' Sekhmet will promise, and an hour later you're still waiting. Regardless of excuses, Sekhmet is hopeless when it comes to estimating how long anything is going to take and as in all aspects of their life, they are easily distracted.

The Sekhmet Partner

Although they are not naturally team-workers, few Sekhmets are happy without a partner to share their life. They need company to be truly content. Consequently, Sekhmets will seldom be without a partner for long. Many settle down early and those who don't will spend as much time as possible with their partner. They are not domineering or possessive, they simply need someone around to give them encouragement and much-needed companionship.

Sekhmets are passionate and uninhibited lovers and give themselves fully to romance. A love of variety and adventure makes Sekhmets exciting and stimulating partners. Although those of this sign are often excessive in their chosen pursuits, they are usually careful with their money. A person expecting endless gifts or expensive nights out from a Sekhmet partner is in for disappointment. Those hoping to 'go Dutch' and share the cost of a date with their Sekhmet is also in for a shock. Sekhmets are not averse to luxury: they just refuse to spend their money in an extravagant or profitless way.

Sekhmet and Other Signs

Affinity Signs

AMUN: The industrious and optimistic Sekhmet is admired by Amun. Both signs have the ability to devote themselves consistently to a single goal or objective.

THE SPHINX: The Sphinx is often cool and relaxed in most situations. The hyperactive Sekhmet seldom disturbs the Sphinx, while the Sphinx's cunning and lively intelligence is much appreciated by Sekhmet. These two signs complement each other nicely, although it may seem to others that Sphinxes and Sekhmets are worlds apart.

SEKHMET: Most Sekhmets enjoy the company of others like themselves. Although they will often be messy or untidy together, they make excellent close friends and partners, sharing a love of excitement and adventure.

ISIS: Isis can take energetic Sekhmet in their stride. Sekhmet often needs a benevolent and controlling hand that Isis is prepared to offer. Almost every attribute lacking in each sign is compensated by the attributes of the other. Some of the most successful partnerships form between Isis and Sekhmet.

Incompatible Signs

HORUS: Energetic Sekhmet and stubborn Horus will often argue and bicker even when they see eye-to-eye.

ANUBIS: Sekhmets and Anubis people share creative traits. However, the headstrong Anubis can often clash with the fiery temperament of Sekhmet. Neither is prepared to give way to the other.

SHU: Sekhmet's energetic mentality is fascinating, though exhausting, to peace-loving Shu.

Compatibility with Other Signs

OSIRIS: Sekhmets like to commit themselves to long-term relationships. Osiris is quickly irritated by anything that becomes routine or lacks variety.

THE PHOENIX: Both Sekhmet and the Phoenix are signs of extreme optimism and get on like a house on fire – after all, they are both creatures of fire. Unfortunately, together they tend to lack restraint: the Phoenix and Sekhmet can find themselves in difficult situations that are hard to resolve.

THOTH: Thoth admires Sekhmet's optimism and determination, although Thoth may become frustrated by Sekhmet's abrupt changes of plans and their failure to see the obvious.

HATHOR: Relationships between Hathors and Sekhmets are particularly volatile. They may adore one another, sharing a love of adventure, travel and excitement. When together, however, both can find their emotions too readily stimulated and arguments may ensue. These signs often share a love/hate relationship.

WADJET: Many Wadjets feel that Sekhmets reveal too much about themselves, and some regard this as a weakness. Sekhmets, for their part, may consider that Wadjets lead a far too conventional lifestyle.

Trends and Influences Through the Year

Over the course of the year Sekhmet can expect the following influences to affect their lives during the separate Egyptian sign-phases:

THOTH August 29 – September 27:
This phase is a time of much activity for Sekhmets, but they

should be careful not to overwork. They may become touchy or sensitive concerning the opinions of others. It is, however, an extremely favourable time for sport and other leisure activities.

HORUS September 28 – October 27:
Anything concerning group activities, either social or business in nature, is well placed for Sekhmet during this phase. Sekhmets who take the lead now are likely to find themselves in a fortuitous or profitable situation.

WADJET October 28 – November 26:
Sekhmet and Wadjet are both creatures of fire and, as such, there could be conflicts of interest during this phase. Particularly concerning relationships, Sekhmet should be careful about involving themselves in disputes – they will probably end up the worst off.

SEKHMET November 27 – December 26:
During their own phase many Sekhmets find excitement and adventure, particularly in romance and love. However, Sekhmet is an especially active creature and should take care not to work too hard during this period.

THE SPHINX December 27 – January 25:
The Sphinx is the message-bearer for Sekhmet, and unusual news may arrive in the earlier days of this phase. Sekhmet is still well placed for romance during this period, while new acquaintances – particularly connected with financial matters – are very much on the cards.

SHU January 26 – February 24:
Shu is swift and graceful, while Sekhmet is strong and powerful. Sekhmet may accordingly overwhelm any subtle influence that the Shu phase may bring. During this time, Sekhmets should be particularly attentive to the smaller details of life, lest they overlook important, sometimes obvious possibilities.

ISIS February 25 – March 26:
The Isis phase is a time of new possibilities, and anything Sekhmet has been putting off should be considered during this period. Many Sekhmets find that most things tend to go right for them at this time of year.

OSIRIS March 27 – April 25:
Few Sekhmets will find this phase a time of peace or tranquillity. Domestic circumstances may require much of Sekhmet's attention. If Sekhmets make certain to divide their time equally between work, rest and play, this phase should go by quite favourably.

AMUN April 26 – May 25:
At no other time of the year is Sekhmet more likely to lose patience than during the phase of Amun. Problems in relationships with close friends or relatives may occur because of Sekhmet irritability.

HATHOR May 26 – June 24:
The phase of Hathor is a time when Sekhmets are exceptionally lucky. They should be careful, however, not to overplay their hand. If they know when to call it a day, this period can bring fulfilment in nearly every aspect of Sekhmet's life.

THE PHOENIX June 25 – July 24:
Both the Phoenix and Sekhmet are fire signs in the extreme. During this phase, Sekhmet imagination will be at its most inventive. New projects are likely to succeed due to quick reactions. Romance is especially favoured, and new and exciting relationships are likely to be formed.

ANUBIS July 25 – August 28:
Travel and change of work or location is favoured during the phase of Anubis. If Sekhmet intends to move to a new house, this can be a particularly auspicious time to begin the process.

Similarly, if they are considering a change of job they should profit by looking for new work at this time. If content to stay put, however, it is a favourable period for seeking promotion or expansion.

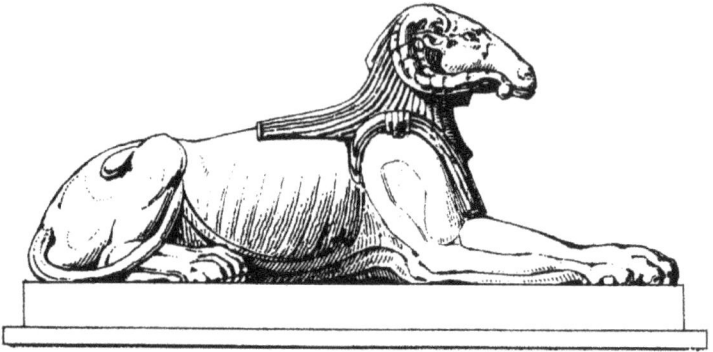

Criosphinx

Hieracosphinx

The Sphinx

None can solve the riddle of the Sphinx,
be he god or mortal man.

Diodurus Siculus, ancient Greek historian.

The Sphinx is the most enigmatic of all the signs. The image of the lion with the head of a human, (and sometimes the wings of a bird), occurs in several mythologies around the world. In Egypt, the sphinx had variations – the criosphinx had the body of a lion and the head of a ram, while the hieracosphinx had the body of a lion and the head of a hawk or falcon.

The name 'sphinx' is a Greek word, and the attributes of this sphinx filtered into Egypt, following the Greek conquest of that land. The Greek sphinx, which was female, posed riddles to any who came across her, and if they failed to answer correctly she'd kill them. In Egyptian mythology, the Sphinx, (whose original Egyptian name was 'Hu'), was not malevolent like its Greek counterpart. It could be male or female – often its statues were given the head of the ruling pharaoh, who could be man or woman. A creature of mystery, it was not only a guardian of temples and treasure, but also a shape-shifter, able to change into the form of any other creature.

Similarly, those born in the sign of the Sphinx share many characteristics with other signs. Sphinxes can modify and adapt their behaviour to suit their present company and current predicament.

Those born in this sign are forever challenging the world around them. They possess a mischievous quality that people sometimes find bewildering, and few but the most perceptive will know the Sphinx's true intentions.

The Sphinx was also a symbol of mystical power, and another remarkable Sphinx trait is uncanny foresight. Often, circumstances will unfold just the way the Sphinx predicted. This unusual ability is due to a deep sense of intuition: an instinctive awareness that would make the Sphinx an excellent detective. They also have the capacity to grasp the root of a problem, possessing shrewd insight into the true cause of difficulties they encounter. Sphinxes are forthright and astute; they have inquiring and probing minds and are remarkably self-disciplined.

Sphinxes are always eager for new experiences and ready to rise to any challenge. However, they do not endeavour to fill their days with so much excitement that they forget about the more practical matters of life. Sphinxes will keep a watchful eye on every detail of their ventures. They can create opportunities from very little and are one of the most enterprising of signs. They seldom, if ever, jump to conclusions and rarely allow prejudice to cloud their judgement. They have patience and accurately gauge the right moment to act.

Positive Qualities

Outwardly the Sphinx is humorous, witty and fun-loving, but inwardly they maintain a serious, sharp-eyed attitude to life. They are ambitious with the capacity to exercise authority, while a strong will and conscientious attitude results in many

Sphinxes holding positions of responsibility. Sphinxes are usually optimistic concerning their chosen ventures, and a keen sense of intuition often brings them success. They have considerable powers of concentration, coupled with manifold technical and artistic skills. Those born in this phase are also extremely self-disciplined, possessing the mental stamina to remain on top of most situations.

Negative Traits

Opportunities are sometimes missed through too great an attachment to outdated ideas or methods. Sphinxes tend to make errors of judgement based on strongly-held opinions. Others may consider Sphinxes to be arrogant or vain at times and may also find Sphinx intuition disturbing. Sphinxes are extremely inquisitive, which can sometimes lead them into trouble. In times of difficulty, they also tend to blame others for problems of their own making.

Appearance

The Sphinx has firm features and a confident and authoritative stature. They usually have a benevolent gaze and exude an aura of self-assuredness. They move with an air of certainty, they carry their heads high and walk with their backs straight. Few are quick or erratic; most being slow and deliberate movers.

Health

The Sphinx is a sign of physical activity and so injuries and broken limbs are common for those born in this phase. Few Sphinxes are worriers and are seldom concerned about their own welfare. Many are inclined to ignore preventative medicine or disregard any tell-tale signs of illness. Repetitive strain injuries, or other ailments that should be tackled early, may be left unattended. This can lead to complications that might easily have been avoided.

Optimising Sphinx Attributes

Sphinxes can be far too cynical at times, refusing to believe anything they have not seen with their own eyes. They are unlikely to take anything at face value or on someone else's word. Sphinxes should try to have a little more faith in human nature. Sphinxes are also eager to know the details of their friends', colleagues' and acquaintances' lives, and are especially intrigued by secrets they become desperate to uncover. By contrast, few Sphinxes will reveal their own motivations or intentions, and certain not their secrets. Sphinxes should learn to give and take a little more, particularly in business or professional matters.

Suitable Occupations

Whatever profession they work in, the Sphinx is generally most successful when self-employed. Sphinxes make especially good entrepreneurs, managers or supervisors. They watch and listen carefully before arriving at conclusions, and only after every angle has been considered. Accordingly, they make solid judgements and sound commercial decisions. Furthermore, they are quick to assert authority firmly and decisively. Being something of a chameleon, and a natural performer, Sphinxes make good actors, or are drawn to careers in the media. Because of their diverse attributes, Sphinxes are found in just about every occupation, and can easily change their employment to a completely different job, should the need arise.

The Sphinx at Work

At work, success is assured, providing colleagues are prepared to let the Sphinx do things their own way. Sphinxes make tough but fair employers, although they may drive their employees a little too hard. They are equally hard on themselves, however, and exercise their many talents with remarkable dedication. They are not easily distracted, able to focus intently upon any given task, and can always be trusted to do any job to the best of their ability. They share common traits with Wadjet, finding it difficult to socialise with close business associates. Many Sphinxes keep their working lives quite separate from their social lives.

The Sphinx Personality

The Sphinx is outgoing, confident and entertaining, and at ease in most company. They love excitement in their lives and can adapt their character and humour to suit the occasion. The Sphinx will fascinate those around them and enjoys being the centre of attention. While Sphinxes tend to be knowledgeable about many subjects, even if they know little of a topic of conversation, they will discuss it in an enlightening and entertaining manner. While being great conversationalists, Sphinxes are also good listeners. People may be enchanted by their eloquent manner and flamboyant personality. They have an enigmatic demeanour that allows them to stand out from the crowd.

The Sphinx enjoys attention and is often envied by others. They like to take a leading role in social activities. People of this sign are always ready to give advice and are prepared to offer comfort to those in distress. However, they prefer to keep their own problems to themselves. Outwardly, Sphinxes might seem unemotional and, unless angered, tend to keep their true feelings private.

Most Sphinxes prefer an ordered environment, although, like Sekhmet, they are more concerned with personal appearance than domestic tidiness. While stylish in appearance, the Sphinx is unlikely to wear outrageous or unusual clothes.

Sphinxes are generally successful in their careers, owing to their capacity to focus fully and use their intuition to make sound decisions. If no one in their working environment seeks to squash or limit them, or hold back their bright ideas, they are helpful members of a team.

Sphinxes tend to divide their time equally between work and leisure activities. They are, however, somewhat ruthless in commercial dealings. The Sphinx expects their competitors and rivals to be as tough as they are. Despite this, the Sphinx is a social creature and loves to make everything as enjoyable as possible for others.

Sphinxes are generally sparing with their deepest affections and expect people to share their sentiments before they are prepared to commit to long-lasting friendships or relationships. To all those who share their life, Sphinxes are fascinating acquaintances.

The Sphinx Parent

Although caring, Sphinx parents are inclined to treat their family like an efficient business concern. They may tend to act like firm but fair employers and expect their children to be exemplary in their behaviour and appearance. They will ensure that their children are well looked after but will tend to concentrate too much on the child's physical welfare. To the Sphinx, health, appearance, good manners and practical achievements often take precedence over a child's emotional needs. Nevertheless, Sphinxes are benevolent and affectionate, wanting the best for their young.

The Sphinx Child

From infancy, the Sphinx child will be responsive to education and eager to learn. Sphinx children are inquisitive in the extreme, wanting to know the reason for everything. They work diligently at school and usually do well in class. There are seldom bad reports of the Sphinx child's academic achievements and most also do well in sport. Many children of this sign are born competitors.

The Sphinx child has a constructive attitude to life, and few born in this phase are likely to be rude, unkind or destructive in any way. They mix well with other children and are polite to adults, though many need constant attention and praise for their achievements. Their leadership qualities develop early, and the little Sphinx will often insist on taking the lead with friends.

The Sphinx Friend

The Sphinx can read situations perfectly. They often have tremendous insight into what is both appealing and popular and can captivate their friends with original and imaginative ideas. The Sphinx is not only a sign of creativity, it is also a sign of communication – many born in this phase make the most entertaining hosts and companions.

Sphinxes have versatility of character and can adapt themselves to most company. Many are natural actors and will assume a personality tailor-made for any occasion. Innate performing skills are a usual Sphinx trait, and many born in this sign fit readily into whatever circumstances surround them. The Sphinx has a firm sense of loyalty, and their close ties to their family need to be accepted by friends and lovers alike.

The Sphinx Partner

The Sphinx is a sign of insight and most born in this phase know precisely the right way to treat a prospective partner. They can readily adapt themselves to saying what others hope to hear and will act to impress. There is nothing false about this remarkable Sphinx versatility. Sphinxes simply enjoy fitting in with others and with the spirit of an occasion.

Sphinxes have silver tongues, and their praise and flattery is hard to ignore. Romantics will find themselves captivated by the magnetic personality of the extroverted, self-assured Sphinx. They can adapt their interests and outlooks on life to suit their lover and are often the most accommodating of partners. Sphinxes hate discord in their domestic lives so much, they will go to tremendous lengths to avoid domestic squabbles or lovers' tiffs. Unless an argument concerns something about which they feel deeply, Sphinxes much prefer to concede defeat for the sake of peace.

Sphinxes have a mysterious, enigmatic quality that others either love or fear. The Sphinx is usually so good at whatever they turn their minds to that they can at times appear somewhat arrogant. This is seldom hollow vanity, rather an assured confidence, which may be misconstrued. Like the enigmatic side of their nature, Sphinx assuredness is either distrusted or admired.

The Sphinx and Other Signs

Affinity Signs

AMUN: The Sphinx is the sign that Amun often admires the most. Their ability to make something out of nothing, together with their keen financial instinct, is greatly respected by Amun.

WADJET: The wise serpent and the cunning Sphinx usually share a common outlook on life and enjoy many of the same interests. Mutual respect, affection and compatibility are often found between these two signs.

SEKHMET: The Sphinx is cool and relaxed in most situations. The hyperactive Sekhmet seldom disturbs the Sphinx, while the Sphinx's cunning and lively intelligence is much appreciated by Sekhmet. These two signs complement each other nicely, although this may puzzle others, who'll assume that Sphinxes and Sekhmets are too different to get on well.

HORUS: Horus and the Sphinx often mix well. The Sphinx has many ideas that they lack the courage to try. Horus is quite prepared to implement the Sphinx's schemes. These signs often make ideal partners.

Incompatible Signs

THOTH: The Sphinx is the sign that Thoth finds hardest to fathom. Their ability to make something out of nothing, and their keen financial sense, are mysteries to Thoth.

ANUBIS: Those born in the Sphinx and Anubis signs often experience a clash or interests and personality. Sometimes they may even distrust one another.

OSIRIS: The meticulous Sphinx can be most annoying to Osiris. The two signs have markedly different temperaments and little in common.

ISIS: Isis is a sign that can solve the Sphinx's eternal riddle. Isis intuition gives them the ability to fathom the motives of those born in the phase of the Sphinx. The Sphinx may find this acutely unnerving.

Compatibility with Other Signs

THE PHOENIX: The Phoenix dislike of financial matters is well compensated for by the Sphinx. The Sphinx is both conservative and thrifty in their approach to life, and the Phoenix respects such attributes in others.

HATHOR: Hathors generally admire the clever Sphinx, and Sphinxes often find the romantic Hathor a stimulating companion.

THE SPHINX: Two Sphinxes tend to compete with one another, each out to get the upper hand. They are not argumentative by nature, and so they may forge successful, although unusual, relationships.

SHU: The openness of Shu is appreciated by the Sphinx and Shu is captivated by Sphinx inscrutability. However, the Sphinx can be a little too overbearing for Shu.

Trends and Influences Through the Year

Over the course of the year the Sphinx can expect the following influences to affect their lives during the separate Egyptian sign-phases:

THOTH August 29 – September 27:
The phase of Thoth brings renewal to the Sphinx. Anything that seems to have reached a stalemate can be rejuvenated by fresh possibilities. If the Sphinx has become bogged down with a problem, the solution could present itself toward the end of this phase. This is an especially favourable time for love, romance and affairs of the heart.

HORUS September 28 – October 27:
If a Sphinx is looking for new employment this is a particularly positive time. Similarly, if the Sphinx is thinking of moving home an opportunity to relocate is very possible.

WADJET October 28 – November 26:
Wadjet acts as the message-bearer for the Sphinx and news from a completely unexpected quarter may be received. The Serpent is a symbol of wisdom, and so the clever Sphinx is particularly astute during this period. Any arguments or disputes are likely to be resolved in the Sphinx's favour.

SEKHMET November 27 – December 26:
Sekhmet's phase is a period favourable to any Sphinx involved in sport or other leisure activities, particularly regarding team events. Any team in which the Sphinx plays a key role is likely to triumph.

THE SPHINX December 27 – January 25:
The Sphinx is a thinker and often needs time to be alone. This is a time for the Sphinx to plan or merely to contemplate. If they keep a balanced perspective, and accept the help of others, solutions to unresolved problems may be discovered.

SHU January 26 – February 24:
The Shu phase is a time when Sphinxes find answers where they least expect to find them. This is also a time of romance and adventure for the Sphinx.

ISIS February 25 – March 26:
The influence of the Isis phase may be detrimental to the Sphinx. A headstrong and inflexible approach can cause problems, particularly in domestic affairs. This may be the best time for the Sphinx to take a vacation.

OSIRIS March 27 – April 25:
This is another phase when Sphinx opportunities are somewhat limited. Relationships may suffer if the Sphinx insists on having the upper hand. Work situations may also suffer if Sphinxes remain inflexible in their approach. However, if they are prepared to see things from others' points of view, then profitable and rewarding changes of direction may result.

AMUN April 26 – May 25:
During the phase of Amun, all the Sphinx's cunning will come into play. It is an especially productive time for business endeavours or matters connected with their professional environment. Promotion at work or recognition for achievements is very likely during this phase. This is also a lucky period generally for the Sphinx, when fortune and chance can go in their favour.

HATHOR May 26 – June 24:
During Hathor's phase, the Sphinx will find acquaintances particularly helpful. If Sphinxes abandon their natural suspicion of strangers, they will find many new avenues open up to them.

THE PHOENIX June 25 – July 24:
In legend, the Sphinx could easily outwit an opponent. Similarly, most born in the Sphinx sign are capable of handling themselves in an argument. The resilient Phoenix, however, can rise majestically from defeat. During this phase, the Sphinx's usual eloquence may lead them nowhere. It is a time of considerable stagnation for them.

ANUBIS July 25 – August 28:
Anubis's phase is auspicious for matters of love in the Sphinx's life. Existing relationships may take on a fresh and interesting dimension, while new love affairs are possible for the Sphinx who is presently single.

Shu

January 26 – February 24

May the breath of Shu bring life to the earth.
May his passing cleanse the sky.

From the Pyramid Texts

Shu is an important figure in one of the Egyptian creation myths. He was the personification of air and the son of the creator god, Atum. (The Egyptians had more than one creator god, and several versions of how the world came into being.) Shu had a divine twin sister, the lioness-headed Tefnut, who was the personification of moisture, dew and rain.

In the hot land of Egypt, the movement of air was regarded as cooling and calming; Shu was a peaceful influence. He is generally represented in human form, with his hieroglyphic sign, an ostrich feather, worn as a head-dress. The feather – and in artistic representations he can wear between one and four – is symbolic of lightness and emptiness. He was also associated with mist, fog and clouds and these nebulous elements were said to be his 'bones'. He was believed to exist between the earth and the sky and was also known as the wind.

Shu and Tefnut had two children, Geb (the earth) and Nut (the sky). In turn, Geb and Nut produced Isis, Osiris, Nephthys, Set and Horus (the elder). Collectively, this family of nine was known as the Ennead.

The Shu person has tremendous creative potential and once their true vocation is realised success is virtually guaranteed. Often, however, they are too self-conscious of their failures and ignore their achievements. When difficulties arise, there is also a strong tendency for Shus to withdraw, occupying themselves with a chosen pursuit, which keeps them apart from others.

Shus are true romantics and love to fantasise and reminisce. Many have the talent to captivate an audience, enlivening conversation by their sheer enthusiasm for romance and adventure. The phrase 'still waters run deep' is often an apt description of Shu. Many give the impression that somewhere within their souls lies myriad divine secrets.

Shus are natural performers and their flamboyant, dramatic personalities never fail to win friends and gain influence. They enjoy a variety of interests and few will remain in the same job or social circumstances for their entire lives. Shus seldom do anything in a conventional style, but lend a showy, theatrical quality to their manifold ventures.

The helpful Shu is a valuable member of any group or team, always eager to help associates and friends. They are like a breath of fresh air, full of innovative ideas. Their individual approach to life is refined with style and panache. Considerate and accommodating, Shus are prepared to lead by example. They hate discord and will avoid pointless quarrels at all costs. They much prefer to see those around them happy and content and will go to great lengths to maintain harmony. They will, however, make a firm stand on behalf of friends, arguing their case with eloquence, while at heart being the peace-maker.

Shus have a close affinity to nature, coupled with a highly developed spirituality. They are compassionate and considerate and will try to alleviate suffering wherever it is found.

Positive Qualities

A cheerful temperament makes most relationships easy for Shus and in general they enjoy considerable popularity. They love social occasions and go out of their way to ensure the pleasure and happiness of others. Their capacity work successfully in whatever profession they choose is well above average, although partners or colleagues are generally required to help with the deeper aspects of administration and investment. Most born in this sign have a deep sense of responsibility, generally sharing a conscientious and principled attitude to life.

Negative Traits

Many Shus miss vital opportunities due to a hesitant and indecisive attitude. Until proved right or successful, Shus can display a lack of confidence, with too great a dependence on the opinions of others. Extravagance and a love of luxury can create financial problems. Sometimes, Shus have unrealistic ideals or aspirations, and disappointments are bound to result. There is also a tendency for Shus to be possessive in relationships.

Appearance

Those born in the sign of Shu usually have long and graceful limbs. Endowed with a fine bone structure, the face of Shu is warm and sensual. Their eyes are bright, alert and expressive, often with long and thick lashes. They are agile, alert and elegant. Shu is a sign of elegance. Some seem almost to float or glide as they walk or have a purposeful yet graceful gait. Most Shu activity is conducted with deliberate and mindful composure: Shus never sprawl or slouch, even when relaxed.

Health

Shu is one of the healthiest of signs. Few born in this phase will suffer from repeated bouts of illness. After childhood, infections of any kind are rare for Shus. Allergies are the most common complaints of this group, resulting in such problems as asthma or hay fever, or food intolerances. Many Shus suffer skin rashes – often the consequence of nervous tension. Anxiety may result in headaches or nausea, particularly if Shu is in severe distress.

Optimising Shu Attributes

The practicalities of life do not always fit well with Shu's imaginative aspirations. Many have an unrealistic attitude to material pursuits and frequently suffer disappointment, due to elevated expectations concerning relationships. Shus have an ingrained sense of humility and are seldom, if ever, arrogant or vain. Admirable though these qualities are, they may result in too much self-sacrifice and a lack of consideration for their own essential needs. Shus should make a determined effort not to let others walk all over them. Those born in this sign are sometimes too kind and generous for their own good.

Suitable Occupations

The caring and understanding Shu works well with the underprivileged, the sick and the elderly. Their sympathetic nature, coupled with a willingness to listen to the problems of others, make counselling, psychology, caring and social work ideal occupations, as well as careers in medicine or nursing. Shus are born communicators, and anything requiring persuasion or direct customer contact are also appropriate professions for Shus. People born in this sign feel close to nature, so many are suited for work involving agriculture, conservation and animal welfare. With a natural flair for the dramatic, many Shus excel in careers concerning music, drama and dance.

The Shu at Work

Shu's amiable disposition makes them popular in the workplace. Colleagues can safely place their trust in them. Anything told to them in confidence is certain to remain a secret. They also provide a sympathetic ear for problems and offer a firm shoulder on which to cry. Kind as they are, the accommodating Shu isn't afraid to speak up on behalf of workmates, who they feel need a champion. They will, however, broach any complaint with considerable diplomacy, refusing to be side-tracked by anger or frustration. They have a capacity to remain calm when tempers flare in others. Therefore, they are extremely helpful to have around when problems and obstacles arise in the workplace.

Shus are diligent and trustworthy workers, capable of intense devotion to duty. They prefer to work in their own way and will excel if they are given ample scope to use their sharp initiative. They are professionally ambitious and strive hard to achieve their objectives. Shus do not work well under pressure, however, with a tendency to become forgetful when stressed.

The Shu Personality

Shu needs to feel good about themselves, and part of their amour in life is their appearance. When wearing their 'armour', they can tackle any situation. Therefore, they devote time and care to their appearance, as well as keeping fit and living healthily. Shus can feel extremely uncomfortable if they don't feel they're looking their best. They prefer to appear elegant and groomed to others. Their armour, their mask, is their defence against the world and they prepare for social encounters as they would for battle. For this reason, some Shus might not like even their closest friends to visit without arranging a time for this in advance.

By contrast, Shu is not as concerned with having a meticulous environment – they're not among the most domesticated of signs. While their homes might be clean, it's often cluttered and untidy. Shu is one of the most forgetful of any sign, forever mislaying their personal possessions.

Shu frequently displays an unorthodox attitude towards life. They live according to their own set of rules and values. However, they are always prepared to help those in distress. They are gracious and generous, excellent listeners and amiable friends. They cannot abide malicious gossip, however, often refusing to continue with a conversation that turns to criticism of anyone not present. They love company and are skilled at hosting events. They might even feel uneasy when alone, except when preparing to meet others. Their physical preparations mirror their emotional preparations, and for that they prefer peace.

Despite their amiability, Shus will not seek to be the centre of attention. If pressed, however, they can take on a role of leadership. They hate inertia, loathe being bored under any circumstances and are always searching for new experiences. Once anything becomes routine, they look for something else to add to their list of interests. Sometimes, they fail to acknowledge their own abilities, lacking faith in their talents and potential. While conscientious at work, at home Shu will often start a task, only to leave it unfinished.

Family life is generally very important to the typical Shu. They fill their lives with love and fellowship. Shus make the most devoted of partners and parents. If they have a secure environment to return to each evening, they will excel in their chosen professions. They will work confidently with colleagues, knowing precisely what others want and how to achieve it. The Shu strength of purpose is strengthened by the knowledge that they are working for the benefit of their family – if they should have one. (And most Shus aren't best content when they haven't.) If they're not giving their very best at work, they feel they're letting their employers and colleagues down.

While some Shus are content to live alone, they generally have a network of friends resembling an extended family outside the home. Without company in their living environment, Shu can be extremely disorganised.

The Shu Parent

Shus are patient and tolerant parents. They do not believe in punishment or severe reprimand of any kind. Instead, they will let their children make their own mistakes, confident that it is the most valuable way for their offspring to learn. Shu parents are affectionate and loving and will encourage their young to the full, always giving the very best of advice. They like their children to be clean and tidy, however, but are rarely angry if they return home dirty or muddy from play. 'Kids will be kids', is usually the motto of the Shu parent. However, because they believe appearances mean so much in life, they'll encourage their children to take care of themselves in this respect.

The Shu Child

The Shu child is sprightly and inquisitive. They are also dreamers and often have invisible childhood friends. Shu children will usually talk to themselves more frequently than those of other signs. That does not mean they do not have real companions: they forge friendships readily and enjoy considerable popularity with other children. They have such vivid imaginations that it is easy for them to create a colourful world of make-believe for others to share.

From an early age, Shu children are bright, alert and quick to learn, although they may require encouragement to perform well in school. Provided a subject is presented in a stimulating fashion, however, the Shu child will take to learning with great enthusiasm. It is up to teachers to make lessons interesting enough for Shu to pay attention.

The Shu Friend

Shus can be wonderful friends; they are excellent listeners and entertaining conversationalists. But they must share a common bond or affinity with someone to enjoy a truly close friendship. They are easy-going and hate to burden anyone with their own troubles. Shus refuse to judge their acquaintances, maintaining an open mind in most situations. They only have one failing as friends: they always mean to keep in touch with those who have moved away, but never seem to get around to it. Eventually, having failed to phone or write, they may even feel guilty and contact may be lost for good.

Shus sometimes seem to exist in an insular, timeless world: they are always late for appointments, hate to be hurried, and insist on doing everything in their own time. When working, thinking or preparing, Shus tend to talk to themselves. They are also garrulous in conversation, forever going off at tangents to the topic being discussed. Strangely enough, this can create a sense of shared reverie, having a remarkably calming influence on those who are anxious, worried or under stress. One always has the feeling that somehow everything will work out for the best after a chat with a Shu friend.

The Shu Partner

Those born in the Shu sign are usually mellow and serene, capable of taking erratic or excitable partners in their stride. They exert a pacifying and calming influence on those in their vicinity. However, Shus are unlikely to be happy near those who expect others to join them in a world of frenzied activity. They prefer to look, listen and learn, offering pertinent advice or comments in their own time of choosing, rather than being swept away with boundless enthusiasm.

The Shu lover is romantic and affectionate, although sometimes a little too sentimental. They are open and giving and willingly offer their trust. They allow themselves to be captivated by those who bring adventure to their lives, providing it is not too disruptive. For Shu to be at their best, they need a stable partner who has a responsible attitude to life. However, for the relationship to be truly successful, their partner must share an imaginative disposition. Anyone who lacks sensitivity is seldom attractive to those born in the Shu sign.

Shu and Other Signs

Affinity Signs

OSIRIS: Shus are generally calm and serene, well able to take the highly-charged Osiris in their stride.

THE PHOENIX: The Phoenix gets on best with those who are less active than they are. Many Shus are calm and serene – at least outwardly. Accordingly, they can exert a positive influence on the Phoenix's impulsive nature.

SHU: The unassuming Shu is usually happy in the company of other Shus. They have many common interests, experience few serious disagreements, and share a deep sense of intuition.

ANUBIS: Anubis's strong family ties and protective instincts can make them ideal partners for Shus. Shus often look at life from a very different perspective to Anubis, and their romantic imagination usually aids Anubis's creativity.

Incompatible Signs

AMUN: Shu is far too sensitive and emotional for Amun, while Amun is too overbearing for Shu. The two signs have little in common, and their outlooks on life differ considerably.

HORUS: The serenity of lifestyle Shu needs is unlikely to be found with a Horus.

SEKHMET: Sekhmet's energetic mentality is fascinating, though exhausting, to the peace-loving Shu.

Compatibility with Other Signs

THOTH: Thoth is often attracted to the openness of Shu, although Thoth can mentally exhaust Shu, who prefers a more serene lifestyle.

HATHOR: Shus and Hathors share an interest in the exotic and unusual aspects of life. Close friendships and relationships are possible, although partnership between these two signs can sometimes suffer due to a lack of practical considerations.

WADJET: Shus and Wadjets have little in common. However, this can sometimes lead to successful partnerships. There is little for them to argue or disagree about.

ISIS: Shus are romantics by nature and may find themselves swept away by Isis panache. Isis's lifestyle is often too dramatic for Shu.

THE SPHINX: The openness of Shu is appreciated by the Sphinx and Shu is captivated by Sphinx inscrutability. However, the Sphinx can be a little too overbearing for Shu.

Trends and Influences Through the Year

Over the course of the year Shu can expect the following influences to affect their lives during the separate Egyptian sign-phases:

THOTH August 29 – September 27:
Thoth brings favourable influences to bear on sporting and leisure activities. At social engagements, Shus will be in their element. Positive developments in Shu's life could result from new acquaintances made during this phase. This is an

especially favourable period for love, romance and affairs of the heart.

HORUS September 28 – October 27:
Shu should be careful not to rush headlong into anything during the phase of Horus. This period, however, can be an excellent time for Shu to take a vacation.

WADJET October 28 – November 26:
Any Shu involved in academic pursuits will find that many achievements are made at this time of year. Shus may find that they are required to learn a new skill to obtain the best results from an important enterprise.

SEKHMET November 27 – December 26:
During the phase of Sekhmet, Shus could have trouble in relationships. They will need their own space, which others may not be prepared to allow them. Shu should stand firm and refuse to be manipulated.

THE SPHINX December 27 – January 25:
The Sphinx is the message-bearer for Shu. Surprise news is likely in the early days of this phase.

SHU January 26 – February 24:
Shu's own phase bring a positive influence for change. A house move or change of job is particularly favourable at this time.

ISIS February 25 – March 26:
During the phase of Isis, Shus might feel they have little control over their own affairs. However hard they try, they seem to get nowhere. It is often best for Shus to wait until this phase is over before they make important decisions.

OSIRIS March 27 – April 25:
The Osiris phase can be a time of laborious activity for Shu. If

lingering problems remain unsolved, this is the best time to act. Shu has an especially practical attitude to life during this period and is well-placed to handle any difficulties that may previously have been avoided.

AMUN April 26 – May 25:
Innovative ideas and intuitive inspiration can open many doors for Shu. This is a favourable time for love and romance. Many Shus meet new partners, get engaged, begin to cohabit, or even get married during an Amun phase.

HATHOR May 26 – June 24:
Shu may find this a somewhat difficult phase to handle. Combined, the influences of Hathor and Shu result in unrealistic or impractical enterprises. This is often a period when financial and domestic problems arise, while business affairs may also suffer.

THE PHOENIX June 25 – July 24:
The firebird brings much excitement to Shu's life. Shus have a deeply romantic temperament and this phase brings many opportunities to meet new people they find attractive, or to have experiences that inspire their spirit.

ANUBIS July 25 – August 28:
This is a phase when Shu is especially lucky, particularly concerning ventures of chance. Business endeavours initiated at this time are likely to succeed and great reward is possible.

Isis

February 25 – March 26

O blood of Isis, bring forth the great magic
that will transform the world.

From The Egyptian Book of the Dead

Usually represented in human form as a beautiful woman, the goddess Isis was known as 'the great of magic'. She was the sister-wife of Osiris and the mother of Horus and was regarded as an ideal of womanhood and motherhood. She was also a goddess of order and wisdom, as well as the symbolic mother of the pharaoh. Her name in Ancient Egyptian was Aset, which meant seat or throne and represented the power of the pharaoh.

Those born in this sign reflect the goddess's qualities, being both practical and intuitive in their approach to life. Isis people can often see things from everyone's point of view. They are endowed with an alert and appealing personality. Although outwardly calm and controlled, they harbour a wealth of inner emotion. Fully prepared to admit fault or error, Isis has little reticence in changing their ideas or tactics should they be proved wrong. Able to accept criticism as an essential part of learning, most born in this sign will consider the opinions of friends and colleagues in all circumstances.

The Isis person will tend to review situations without personal prejudice, seldom choosing sides in disputes. Such qualities permit them to formulate balanced plans and reach level-headed conclusions. Isis will look, listen and learn patiently before deciding upon a course of action. Whether or not they agree with others, Isis will try to appreciate the validity of all arguments. They are always ready to be persuaded – but reasoning must be sound.

Isis is usually honest, forthright and idealistic. Both logic and intuition direct their actions – the perfect blend for success in any undertaking. They are hard-working and blessed with a keen, subtle intelligence, having little difficulty expressing themselves in a clear and eloquent manner. They mix well socially, are easy-going with their acquaintances, and make undemanding friends and helpful colleagues. Isis people display imaginative foresight and have a remarkable aptitude to see things from varying perspectives. They will take all angles of a problem into consideration before arriving at conclusions and are often inspired with revolutionary ideas.

Positive Qualities

Isis people possess an energetic, attractive and lively personality. A flamboyant character and a flair for the dramatic ensure they frequently take centre stage. Confident in most circumstances, they are able to gain an overall perspective on any situation. A mystical inclination, coupled with a highly-developed sense of intuition, turns many born in this sign toward philosophical or spiritual pursuits. Isis people are creative thinkers, having many unique and individual ideas. They are imaginative and adaptable, and their sense of humour guarantees them social success.

Negative Traits

Isis people have vivid imaginations, and should problems become too serious they tend to retreat into a world of make-believe. Lofty ideas can reduce the chances of success in practical ventures, while unrealistic expectations can cause disappointment. Wishful thinking can also be a danger when dealing with difficult situations. Sometimes tactless, those born in this sign often speak their mind too readily.

Appearance

Isis eyes are wide and expressive. Many born in this sign also have high foreheads and often a well-defined widow's peak. They have quick reactions, although most move in an unhurried but graceful manner. Everything Isis does is undertaken with an appearance of calculated accuracy. Even when they're relaxed, their bodies will appear ready and alert.

Health

Isis's intense commitment to their projects and activities may result in anxiety and other stress-related problems. However, they regulate their lives in such a fashion that they are unlikely to suffer from gastronomic complaints or stomach trouble. One beneficial aspect of their physiology is the capacity to heal or recover rapidly from injury. Broken bones mend quickly and cuts and bruises are swift to heal.

Optimising Isis Attributes

Idealists by nature, some born in this sign may prefer to live in a world of reverie, even fantasy, if problems become too serious. They may retreat from the dismal, uninviting world and become reserved, secretive and detached. In such circumstances, Isis should face reality and realise that everything is not always going to work out for the best. Another Isis drawback is a tendency toward compulsive devotion to work. They may dedicate themselves so entirely to a heartfelt cause that relationships, family life and everyday matters are neglected. Isis should remain aware of the potentially obsessive side to their character.

Suitable Occupations

A thirst for knowledge draws many born in this sign into academic careers. Their adventurous, enquiring minds suit the world of scientific research. Isis has an excellent eye for detail, so photography, painting, sculpture, architecture and commercial art are also ideal occupations for many born in this sign. Isis enjoys the limelight. Whether actors, entertainers or professional persuaders, Isis accurately gauges public reaction, captures attention and moulds opinion with considerable ease. Many successful advertising executives are born in this phase.

The Isis at Work

Isis has a flexible attitude to work. Their ability to see things from everyone's point of view ideally suits them for positions of responsibility. The Isis employer is a fair, conscientious and hard-working boss, while the Isis employee mixes well with colleagues. Few born in the Isis sign are found entangled in professional squabbles. They make excellent mediators, helping to solve any problems that arise in their place of work. Isis's occupation must offer challenge and scope for initiative. If a job lacks stimulation or creative potential, Isis will soon grow bored and lose interest entirely. Until a fulfilling career is found, few born in this sign will remain content with a job for long.

The Isis Personality

Isis is the most socially versatile of signs. They can converse knowledgably at any level, whether at a formal dinner with high-ranking colleagues or in a local bar with casual friends. They possess a firm set of ideals and, no matter how unconventional they may appear to others, they will defend their beliefs and opinions with zeal. Isis is quick to condemn any signs of inequality or injustice in the way they or others are treated. They are not afraid to confront people in public if they feel it's warranted.

Isis makes a devoted friend, colleague and partner, although they might sometimes seem distant or preoccupied. They can also be changeable in temperament, one minute fully engrossed in conversation, the next detached in a world of thought. People must learn to accept them the way they are. Despite appearances, Isis's occasional withdrawal from a conversation doesn't necessarily indicate bad feeling or disagreement; out of the blue, an idea completely removed from the current topic may simply have occurred to them that requires (for them) immediate pondering.

All Isis people tend to adopt an unconventional style of dress, whether it's complete outfits, or eccentric details in accessories that signify their quirky tastes. Even if they're interested in current fashions, or need to dress formally for work, they will always make an individual statement in their chosen attire. It may be no more than an unusual piece of jewellery. Look closely and somewhere about Isis you will find their unique personal trademark – such as a watch or a piece of jewellery of unusual design.

Periods of privacy are of utmost importance to Isis and they will defend their right to them with passion. They might also exhibit unorthodox behaviour in some situations, when their manner and motives remain inscrutable and complex. By contrast, Isis is endlessly fascinated by the intentions and motivations of others. Whether it's friends, lovers, or mere acquaintances, Isis is determined to discover just what it is that makes them tick. Isis therefore has a paradoxical, enigmatic personality that many find enchanting.

Isis is usually attracted to those who lead interesting or exotic lifestyles. At the very least, friends and lovers must share an unusual approach to life. They are kind and generous to their partners, who must accept that Isis people will insist upon having their own personal space – they hate invasion of their private thoughts and contemplations. However, they seldom have anything to hide; they simply need to retreat from time to time. Mental solitude enables them to solve not only their own problems but those of others.

The Isis Parent

Isis parents will encourage their children to think for themselves and stand on their own two feet. Encouraging their offspring's education in daily life, they bring school subjects to life by injecting them with flair and imagination, making learning a more stimulating activity. Few born in this sign insist that their children adopt their own interests or values; neither will they reprimand their young without a fair hearing. Isis parents will listen to their children with an open mind, before passing judgement on their motives or actions.

The Isis Child

From infancy, Isis children are dreamers. They have lofty ambitions and their hearts overflow with expectation. Isis children question constantly the world about them, only satisfied when they have learned all about the myriad subjects and items that grab their attention. Consequently, the young Isis may lack concentration when asked to apply themselves exclusively to a subject at school – particularly if the subject isn't that interesting to them. They have a thirst for knowledge but prefer to pursue it in their own way. When they apply themselves, however, they are immensely creative achievers.

Physical activity is not high on their list of priorities, even if they do have the physique to excel at sport. The Isis child much prefers to work alone rather than as part of an organised group or team.

The Isis Friend

While amiable with others, Isis is comfortable with their own company, and balk at being drawn into any type of close-knit or elite community. They dislike conformity and prefer to remain an elusive but prominent figure in the crowd. Isis enjoys socialising – they can be extremely witty, humorous and fun-loving – but they hate to confine themselves to one set of standards or principles. Everything has its place in Isis philosophy, and everyone has the right to their own opinions and lifestyle. Anyone who is dogmatic, inflexible or stuck in a rut is unlikely to be Isis's friend. More than anything else, Isis despises prejudice or injustice of any kind.

Isis often has trouble making long-term friends, despite their engaging and magnetic personality. They are usually so different from others that they find it impossible to share continual enthusiasm for the same old routines. Once they do meet someone with whom they share a common outlook, Isis can cast an irresistible spell on their new-found friend, leading them into a world of wonder and excitement. Furthermore, Isis will do all in their power to protect those they love, sacrificing themselves should the need arise.

The Isis Partner

Younger Isis people often have unrealistic expectations of their chosen partners and this can lead to bitter disappointment. Eventually their attitude will adapt itself to reality and they'll adopt an ability to compromise and to accept people as they are.

Once committed, Isis will be a devoted and passionate lover, although public displays of affection are rare. Successful partnerships involve Isis being allowed to retain their individualism and personal freedom. Isis is averse to interference in their affairs, no matter by whom or however well intended.

Occasionally Isis will seek temporary escape from the world. At such times they will retreat and contemplate in solitude. Partners can sometimes take this the wrong way, mistakenly believing that they have done something to offend, or that it means their partner is losing interest in them. But provided Isis is left to sort out their problems alone, they will soon resume their normal behaviour.

Isis and Other Signs

Affinity Signs

THE PHOENIX: Those born in the Phoenix phase find themselves attracted to the exotic or unusual. Isis is perhaps the most intriguing of signs, and their idiosyncratic style is irresistible to the Phoenix.

HATHOR: Hathors are often attracted to unconventional Isis, while Isis moves towards those with imagination. These signs are most compatible, and many successful relationships and business partnerships result.

WADJET: Wadjet's love of learning is much respected by Isis. Wadjet finds Isis's unique insight equally fascinating. The two signs work well together, and partnerships are often successful.

SEKHMET: Isis can take energetic Sekhmet in their stride. Sekhmet often needs a benevolent and controlling hand, which Isis is prepared to offer. Almost all attributes lacking in both signs are compensated by the other, and some of the most successful partnerships are formed between Isis and Sekhmet.

Incompatible Signs

ISIS: Few born in this phase are at ease in the company of others who share their sign. Isis's life is often too unusual to be spent so close to another who has similarly unconventional attitudes.

THE SPHINX: Isis can solve the Sphinx's eternal riddle. Isis's intuition gives them the ability to fathom the motives of those born in the phase of the Sphinx. The Sphinx may find this acutely unsettling.

ANUBIS: Isis can unnerve Anubis. Few Anubis people like ideas as unconventional as many born in the Isis phase may have.

Compatibility with Other Signs

OSIRIS: Isis needs their own space. The Osiris desire to be a part of everything in their friends' or partner's life is often too much for Isis to put up with. Nevertheless, in Egyptian mythology, Isis and Osiris were partners. As such, both can make considerable efforts to overcome their differences and long-lasting relationships are possible.

THOTH: Although Isis and Thoth mix well socially, close relationships or working partnerships can suffer. When together, people of these two phases tend to behave irresponsibly.

AMUN: Amun admires the resourceful Isis, but Isis often finds Amun far too conventional in their approach to life.

HORUS: As both Horus and Isis commit themselves so completely to a chosen pursuit, these two signs work well together if they share a similar, heart-felt interest. If their interests lie in different directions, however, they are unlikely to have the time to spare for one another.

SHU: Shus are romantics by nature and may find themselves swept away by Isis panache. Isis's lifestyle is often too dramatic for Shu.

Trends and Influences Through the Year

Over the course of the year Isis can expect the following influences to affect their lives during the separate Egyptian sign-phases:

THOTH August 29 – September 27:
This is a particularly favourable period for romantic affairs. Many Isis people first meet their future partners during this phase. In business, Thoth brings new opportunities for prosperity.

HORUS September 28 – October 27:
Domestic matters are likely to play a key role in the life of Isis people during this phase, and the home may need more attention than usual. This is a period of good luck concerning ventures of chance.

WADJET October 28 – November 26:
During the phase of Wadjet, Isis could find themselves inadvertently drawn into problems over which they have no control.

SEKHMET November 27 – December 26:
Energetic Sekhmet influences Isis positively. This is a particularly favourable time for sport and leisure activities. Isis people engaged in competition are especially likely to fare well.

THE SPHINX December 27 – January 25:
During the phase of the Sphinx, Isis may acquire something they have long sought, only to discover it is not as they expected.

SHU January 26 – February 24:
Shu brings social success for Isis. If Isis attends a special occasion during this phase they could be in for a pleasant surprise.

ISIS February 25 – March 26:
During their own phase, Isis is often inspired by unique and original ideas. Projects initiated during this period have far-reaching consequences. A change of lifestyle may be initiated.

OSIRIS March 27 – April 25:
The phase of Osiris is a time of reflection and contemplation for Isis. Outstanding problems may be resolved through Isis intuition. A new acquaintance may alter the course of Isis's life.

AMUN April 26 – May 25:
This is the phase when travel is favourable. Any Isis seeking a change of home or occupation should discover new opportunities.

HATHOR May 26 – June 24:
The phase of Hathor is a time for Isis to plan. Any idea formulated during this time should lead to success. The influences of Hathor can easily be directed and channelled by the celestial Isis. Any Isis seeking new relationships, especially in romance, could find this period particularly favourable.

THE PHOENIX June 25 – July 24:
During the Phoenix phase, Isis often experiences their greatest difficulties. Isis prefers something to end before something else begins. A situation Isis had considered over and done with may return to their lives. An unwelcome connection with the past could open old wounds.

ANUBIS July 25 – August 28:
Anubis and Isis work hand in hand to ensure success. This is a phase when hard work can finally pay off. Anubis is also the message-bearer for Isis, and surprise news is likely toward the end of this phase.

Isis and Osiris

Osiris

March 27 – April 25

O Osiris, the eternally good, the perfect one,
he who sits in the place of the all-seeing eye.
From The Pyramid Texts

Depicted in green-skinned human form, with the insignia of rulership – the crook and flail – across his chest, Osiris was the god of the Underworld and the afterlife, where he was regarded as a just and merciful judge. He also presided over resurrection and regeneration. As Lord of the Underworld, he was believed to be responsible for the creation of life, including the sprouting of vegetation and the annual inundation of the Nile. His name in Ancient Egyptian was Asar.

One of the Ennead of Heliopolis, (the family of gods associated with the Heliopolitan creation myth), Osiris was the son of Geb and Nut and the brother-wife of Isis. Another of his siblings, the god of chaos, Set, fought with him and in the battle Osiris was dismembered. The parts of his body were scattered around

Egypt. Isis undertook many adventures to recover all these parts and reassemble him. One of his cult centres was at Abydos, in Middle Egypt, where the Oseirion, the temple dedicated to him, remains.

Like the inundating and receding waters of the Nile, those born in this sign tend to be elusive. Osiris is sometimes misunderstood, and their emotions are a mystery. They are highly active, and, like the ever-flowing waters of the river, those born in this phase rarely allow themselves to be restricted.

Most Osiris people are energetic and quick-witted and have a strong compulsion to keep on the move. Curious by nature, they show considerable interest in their friends' affairs and are ever ready to help others or intercede on their behalf. They are perhaps the most inquisitive of any sign – Osiris hates to feel excluded. They are not natural followers and have an idiosyncratic style all their own.

Those born in this phase have the capacity to retain a wealth of information. Even when they are discussing something of which they have little knowledge, they can make themselves appear to be experts. Osiris is eager to impress and refuses to admit ignorance on any subject. They have a lively imagination and an ability to make life interesting for everyone who knows them.

Osiris is a sign of communication, and many born in this phase share a love of language. They are voracious readers, and are erudite and eloquent, with the ability to express themselves in a vivid and witty manner. They have a marvellous sense of humour, although it is seldom zany or surreal. Neither is their humour unkind. They are unlikely to appreciate a joke at someone else's expense. Osiris people are natural communicators, and others may find themselves captivated by their tales and anecdotes. Many Osiris people are excellent speakers, with a natural ability to entertain and encourage others.

Positive Qualities

Osiris people have an active intellect, together with a keen sense of intuition. Self-reliance and determination play an important part in ensuring their success in life. Osiris' natural charm is guaranteed to arouse the interest of prospective romantic partners. Those of this sign have a highly energetic personality, coupled with acute powers of observation. Most are charitable and altruistic, although sometimes eccentric in their ways. They are fast on the uptake, quick to seize the initiative, and are always eager for new experiences. Many are avidly interested in music and drama.

Negative Traits

Often misunderstood, there is sometimes a tendency for Osiris to avoid commitments and responsibilities. An intense dislike of bureaucracy, along with a refusal to conform to tradition, sometimes results in avoidable complications in their lives. Although often gifted with a quick sense of humour, they are inclined to be cynical. Osiris also lacks tact when dealing with those they feel to be in the wrong.

Appearance

Energetic by temperament, Osiris seldom keeps still. They are particularly prone to gesticulating with their hands. Even on the phone, they make exaggerated gestures to emphasise a point or demonstrate what they are saying. Osiris is restless and fidgety, seldom seeming relaxed. When thinking, they are apt to fiddle with small objects around them.

Health

Osiris people are worriers, which may sometimes be detrimental to their health. Allergies and ailments related to the nervous system are common complaints. Not ones for routine, Osiris people have irregular eating habits and often skip meals. The positive effect is that they seldom have a weight problem.

Alternatively, such a lifestyle can play havoc with their digestive systems. Osiris people dislike small or confined spaces and may suffer from claustrophobia: they particularly hate elevators or dark and tiny rooms.

Optimising Osiris Attributes

Osiris people are noted for their adaptability and versatility. However, they tend to lack a singleness of purpose, and powers of concentration need deliberate cultivation. Otherwise, even though they have more creative potential than many other signs, they may not make the most of their talents. Osiris people generally spread themselves too thin, in many different directions at once, and often fail to follow through with plans they start. As soon as a project or event is under way, another, more interesting challenge might be eagerly accepted. Osiris people should make longer-term plans – and stick to them.

Suitable Occupations

Osiris people have keen powers of observation and are quick to learn. They are well-suited for occupations that require fast reactions. They are not ideal candidates, however, for work necessitating prolonged periods of intense concentration. They grow restless far too quickly. Teaching appeals to Osiris people, as does anything connected with the media. They are excellent talkers and are in their element as salespeople. They are not the best of listeners, however, and if they work in a job involving sales they may fail to realise when they are falling short of persuading a potential customer. They usually compensate for this by the sheer volume of work they can get through.

Osiris people are happier in the open, away from formal places of work. They prefer travelling to sitting behind a desk, or working in a confined space, and they dislike the restrictions of the office environment. Similarly, in manual trades, they work best out on site. Osiris people can turn their hands to most endeavours, and intricate or inventive work suits them well.

The Osiris at Work

Osiris is a conscientious worker. They are good organisers, although their individual places of work might be piled high with clutter – a constant reminder of their busy schedule. They can work on several tasks simultaneously and are particularly industrious employees. As employers, or in a managerial role, they make a firm stand on major decisions. On lesser issues, they are somewhat changeable, continually updating their strategy. Employees or fellow workers can be left confused by such tactics. All the same, the Osiris approach is one of adaptability that usually reaps rewards.

As fellow workers, they are not always the easiest people with whom to get along. Some may find Osiris inquisitiveness annoying. They are always eager to keep up with gossip and sometimes say more than they should. But they can be tremendous fun to be around, making the most laborious activities seem interesting.

The Osiris Personality

Osiris is not a strongly-domesticated creature. They would prefer to pay someone else to attend to what they regard as tedious, time-wasting chores in the home. They do like a comfortable environment, however, so if they can't afford the services of a cleaner, will undertake the work themselves, if somewhat untidily. However, even in the midst of disorder, they always know precisely where everything is within the jumble around them.

Osiris enjoys entertaining and welcomes visitors warmly into their home. If they offer sumptuous food to their guests, however, it's unlikely they cooked it themselves. Their usual attitude is: 'take me as you find me'. Osiris dislikes being dependent on others, and while their environment might appear disorderly, Osiris will treat the running of their home as an efficient business. They will ensure their finances are kept in order.

Osiris has a sweet, childish air that is particularly attractive to potential partners. They are considerate and treat everyone as equals. Most of them fall for people with strong personalities, sometimes much older than themselves. They are blessed with great charm and can turn this on and off at will. Osiris people are generous with compliments, flattering those around them. They are gifted with a quick or dry sense of humour and are always ready with a witty or pertinent remark.

Those born in this sign usually have a frivolous attitude to life. When annoyed, however, they can be extremely sarcastic. In fact, this is their usual means of defence. As a rule, Osiris is a peace-maker and unlikely to resort to physical outbursts. They can use their dexterity with words as a weapon if needed, and this is generally their preferred way of dealing with conflict. It's unlikely they'd ever strike out in exasperation or anger. This said, they can have a hot temper but, if so, will be inclined to take out their frustration on inanimate objects. They find a noisy way to express their anger, which releases tension.

The Osiris Parent

Osiris people are perhaps the most exciting parents for any child to have. Osiris loves to be involved with their children's games. They join in the fun wholeheartedly and are forever thinking up adventurous pastimes for their young. Holidays can be full of adventure. The Osiris parent is young at heart and goes out of their way to follow – or at least understand – their children's lifestyles as they mature. They take a keen interest in their children's activities – being especially fond of shared outdoor activities. Sometimes children of an Osiris may find themselves embarrassed by their parent's enthusiasm and youthful outlook on life, especially in front of their friends.

The Osiris Child

Children born in this phase are quick to learn, generally learning to read at an early age, often before school. When they start going to school, Osiris children are often remarkable achievers, although they can bring problems for teachers. There will be few complaints concerning academic ability, but school reports may repeatedly criticise Osiris's lapses of concentration. The problem for many Osiris children is that they have usually understood what's being taught early on; they have simply grown restless and irritable while other children take time to catch up. Osiris is also a worrier and sometimes examination results may suffer. As they are exceptionally keen to do well, children of this sign often overtax themselves with academic work.

Osiris people are likely to succeed in life much earlier than many other signs. Many child prodigies are born in this phase. Their success in later life, however, depends very much upon controlling their inclination to chop and change the nature of their work. Osiris people find it hard to stick to anything for long, especially once it has become a familiar routine.

The Osiris Friend

Osiris hates to pass up a challenge and will often drop other commitments to pursue a new opportunity. On the other hand, those born in this phase are the first to draw attention to the inconsistency of others. Another handicap for Osiris is a tendency to become embroiled in petty details. Do not try arguing with Osiris; it will get you nowhere – except into a state of confusion. Osiris will leave you skilfully side-tracked, just when you think you have proved a point.

Occasionally, Osiris people show signs of jealousy or of being offended, but this is usually only a temporary reaction. With frequently changing interests, they are quick to forget. If you feel you've somehow upset your Osiris friend, your natural inclination might be to apologise. This usually isn't worth the bother. By the time you've decided on what to say, Osiris will probably have already forgotten about the issue. The best attitude to adopt with Osiris people is to live and let live.

The Osiris Partner

Others will always know when Osiris is annoyed. Partners will notice how they move noisily around the house, banging furniture or slamming doors. Sometimes, they form deep attachments, at other times they move from one relationship to another with careless lack of concern. It may seem that they will never settle down, then suddenly and unexpectedly, they might announce they are about to marry or move in with someone. Generally, once the choice is made, they will work hard to ensure a lasting partnership – that is, provided their partner is prepared to accommodate Osiris's manifold interests.

If a partner strongly disagrees with Osiris's activities, the ideal strategy is to give it time. Before long, Osiris usually finds something else to do and quickly loses interest in many hobbies or activities they take up. Osiris people hate to be pressured. The best way to handle them is to air your objections calmly, then let the subject drop.

Osiris people enjoy romantic evenings that involve great attention to detail. They excel at dinner-table conversation, and love to buy their partners gifts. Osiris is one of the best signs with whom to share a date.

In domestic life, they can be somewhat irritating, however. For example, they might quibble and argue when choices must be made in the home, or when appliances or vehicles must be purchased. They always want the best value but have difficulty deciding what that is. Even when they finally make up their minds, they tend to complain later that they should have made a different decision.

Quite often, Osiris is more comfortable living apart from their lovers, especially in early life. They don't like having demands made of them and would never conform to the idea of a traditional home-maker. This doesn't mean Osiris can't be a devoted lover. When they do find someone they feel they could actually live with, they will compromise sufficiently to make the partnership work.

Osiris and Other Signs

Affinity Signs

SHU: Many born in the Shu phase are calm and serene, well able to take the highly-charged Osiris in their stride.

ANUBIS: Anubis people are prepared to give others their own space – something Osiris desperately needs. Unlike some signs, Anubis is has no problem with Osiris inquisitiveness and is prepared to 'bare all' to satisfy them.

HORUS: Both signs are particularly tolerant of one another. Horus's shortcomings are like Osiris's own, such as escaping wherever possible from tiresome responsibilities. Both hate to be tied down. With so many interests, Horus is seldom in conflict with Osiris.

OSIRIS: With a great deal of shared interests and compatible traits, Osiris is unlikely to find themselves in conflict with others of the same sign.

Incompatible Signs

THOTH: Thoth values privacy too much to be constantly around Osiris. Osiris often finds fault with Thoth changeability. Osiris people themselves are changeable, but in interests and activities: Thoth is changeable in temperament.

HATHOR: Hathor is too sentimental for Osiris. Hathor seeks close relationships and has a need for firm, emotional commitments. Osiris feels too restricted by such demands.

THE SPHINX: The meticulous Sphinx can be most annoying to Osiris. The two signs have markedly different temperaments and little in common.

Compatibility with Other Signs

ISIS: Isis needs personal space. Osiris's desire to be a part of everything in their partner's life is often too much for Isis's liking. Nevertheless, in Egyptian mythology, Isis and Osiris were partners. As such, if both try to overcome their differences strong relationships are possible.

WADJET: Wadjet and Osiris mix well enough, although close relationships are rare. Wadjets are too pragmatic and take life too seriously for Osiris. Many Wadjets consider Osiris to be irresponsible.

SEKHMET: Sekhmets like to commit themselves to long-term endeavours. Osiris is quickly irritated by anything that becomes routine or lacks variety.

THE PHOENIX: The Phoenix and Osiris often work well together, although in relationships the Phoenix usually seeks consistency, which is generally lacking in Osiris's life.

AMUN: These two signs often have many interests in common. However, Osiris hates to be told what to do. Amun is sometimes too authoritative for Osiris's liking.

Trends and Influences Through the Year

Over the course of the year Osiris can expect the following influences to affect their lives during the separate Egyptian sign-phases:

THOTH August 29 – September 27:
Thoth is a phase of swift activity, and the typical Osiris is a quick thinker. As Thoth and Osiris are both are highly changeable by nature, Osiris should be careful of making snap decisions during this period.

HORUS September 28 – October 27:
Horus represents risk and courage, which is favourable for Osiris speculation. This is a phase of adventure for Osiris, and affairs of the heart can move in a positive direction. This phase also favours advantageous meetings and important new acquaintances.

WADJET October 28 – November 26:
Plans for change are best implemented during this phase. Any Osiris seeking a new job or change of location may discover exciting possibilities.

SEKHMET November 27 – December 26:
The influence of fire-breathing Sekhmet tends to evaporate the positive influences of the watery Osiris. Plans can be dashed and hopes and aspirations may fade. Osiris should tread carefully in domestic affairs; an innocent remark could be taken the wrong way.

THE SPHINX December 27 – January 25:
An intriguing mystery may confront Osiris during the phase of the riddle-guarding Sphinx. The Sphinx may also bring financial reward. It is a particularly lucky time for Osiris people, especially concerning games or sporting activities.

SHU January 26 – February 24:
The phase of high-flying Shu is often a time of travel for Osiris. It is a good time for a vacation or weekend away. Shu is the message-bearer for Osiris, so this phase is also a time for favourable news.

ISIS February 25 – March 26:
This is a time for the unusual or unexpected. A word of warning, however – Osiris should avoid taking everything at face value.

OSIRIS March 27 – April 25:
During their own phase, Osiris people should be careful not to overwork. This is a time when haste could jeopardise work plans or result in errors of judgement concerning finances. In matters of love and romance, however, Osiris may be pleasantly surprised.

AMUN April 26 – May 25:
Amun is a sign of achievement in material affairs. It also represents steady progress – requiring patience – and patience is not an Osiris virtue. Osiris people should not give up if something seems hopeless or slow in development. There is probably far more headway being made than they realise.

HATHOR May 26 – June 24:
The Hathor phase can be a time of intense activity for Osiris people. They are more single-minded than at any other time of the year. This is usually a period of reward, when new opportunities are recognised and seized. The influence of Hathor can augment the possibility of remarkable success. It is also a positive period for any Osiris seeking romance.

THE PHOENIX June 25 – July 24:
Osiris is a sign of fast, mercurial energy. The Phoenix is also a sign of rapidity, bringing progress for many Osiris people.

ANUBIS July 25 – August 28:
Osiris people may find themselves entangled in quarrels or experience difficulty in relationships during the phase of Anubis.

Amun with Four Ram Heads

Amun

April 26 – May 25

O Amun, hidden one, he who abides in all things,
he who rules over all.

From an inscription at the Temple of Karnak

History has left us more records concerning Amun than many of the other Egyptian gods. A creator god, his veneration became almost a kind of monotheism in the New Kingdom (between the 16th and 11th centuries BC), and in the Late Kingdom (664-332 BC) he was adopted as the supreme state deity. Other gods were said to be manifestations of him; he was the King of Gods.

Amun was adopted as the patron deity of the city of Thebes and eventually became fused with the sun god, Ra (or Re) to become Amun-Ra. His wife was the goddess Amaunet and his son the moon-god Khonsu. Amun was sometimes represented with the head of a ram and sometimes in completely human form. His symbols were the criosphinx, or ram-headed sphinx, and the two huge feathers that make up his head-dress in most artistic representations. His name meant 'the hidden one' or 'the invisible one'. He was the highest creator god, who brought the cosmos into existence, creating the earth and sky from the power of his thoughts.

Those born in this sign are strong and resolute, to whom others look for guidance. The Amun person, however, can often fail to understand those less strong than themselves, finding it incomprehensible that the tasks they find easy others may find hard. They make excellent leaders, if they remember not to overtax those who work for and with them. When left without a challenge, Amun may lapse into a state of lethargy, content to watch the world go by. They are not the best people to come up with ideas for a new project, although once it's underway Amun leadership traits afford an invaluable contribution towards success. Therefore, they work best with a team of creative people to supervise.

Particularly conscientious, Amun often plays a leading role in political organisations or social groups. Few born in this sign are inclined to do anything on the spur of the moment and most are averse to change. Amun forms firm opinions and convictions. Anything they set their mind to has a very good chance to succeed. They have a practical attitude to life and are seldom ones for dreaming, reminiscing or fantasising. Amun is a realist and most born in this sign have an abundance of common sense.

Amun is especially patient, and most apply themselves with unflagging diligence to any enterprise. In business matters, Amuns make excellent spokespeople, able to negotiate the best bargain. They are not, however, the ideal sign for initiating new ventures, as they are often suspicious of the risks involved.

Experimentation is not an Amun trait, and most born in this sign are reluctant gamblers.

Positive Qualities

Amuns have exceptional powers of leadership and their strong willpower is matched by excellent executive skills. With a considerable aptitude for making money, Amun is always willing to devote time and effort towards the success of an enterprise. Strongly principled, they often possess great courage and are reliable and trustworthy. With much physical vitality, they usually enjoy robust health, coupled with a love of sport, action and outdoor activities.

Negative Traits

An overbearing attitude may reduce the chances of social success, while a headstrong temperament, coupled with intolerance, can lead to conflict. Amuns may make errors of judgement due to strongly-biased opinions. Many Amuns have unrealistic expectations of others. A stubborn adherence to ideas can make certain relationships difficult. Sometimes Amun can be arrogant and overbearing.

Physical Appearance

Those born in this sign are often sturdy in appearance, have firm features and a confident and authoritative stature. Amun tends to look you straight in the eye and has a powerful countenance. While Amun is a sign of activity, it is not a sign of nervous energy. There may therefore be a tendency for those born in this phase to become overweight, particularly in later life.

Health

Throat infections are common for those born in this sign, especially in childhood, when frequent bouts of tonsillitis, and other disorders of the throat and neck, are not uncommon. As Amun is a physically active type, injuries and broken limbs are frequent amongst this group. Those born under other signs may be slim, even skinny, no matter what their lifestyle. Amun, however, needs to make a concerted effort regarding diet and exercise to remain trim.

Optimising Amun Attributes

Amuns are often over-cautious and share a stubborn reluctance to take chances. They may be highly competent organisers and administrators, but experimentation and risk-taking is best left to others. Sometimes their hesitancy can be a handicap: frequently they fail to exploit their capabilities or realise their full potential. They often become set in their ways, finding it difficult to adapt to new situations. For the best results, Amun should learn to take occasional risks and realise that failures are often an important part of learning.

Suitable Occupations

Amuns prefer careers offering steady advancement and long-term security. Their innate patience sees them through times of difficulty, usually leading to supervisory or managerial roles in their chosen line of work. Those born in this phase are good with money, so financial careers are particularly suitable. Amuns make excellent accountants, although work involving financial speculation is not the forte of the cautious Amun.

While not overly artistic or creative, or naturally inclined to 'perform', Amuns are usually successful in whatever occupation they choose. They make sensible and responsible decisions in management and are conscientious workers. Amun is a versatile sign regarding employment, and most born in this phase are quite capable of learning almost any trade.

The Amun at Work

Amun is a sign of fixed character: few born in this phase have adaptable personalities. If a change in outlook or direction is required in their working environment, Amun might find it hard to adapt. Amuns are consistent in their habits and behaviour and pursue professional objectives with unfaltering application and dedication. They make the most steadfast of colleagues, and fellow workers generally know exactly where they stand with them. They are easy enough to get along with during working hours but, as with a few other signs, Amuns like to draw a strict dividing line between working and social life. Often their personal friends are from an entirely separate circle of acquaintances to their colleagues at work.

The Amun Personality

Amun can be either an industrious career person or a committed home-maker. Unlike some signs, however, they might find difficulty mixing the two. The happiest Amun is often the one who has devoted their life to one or the other. Most Amuns are uncomfortable if they're required regularly to 'change hats' during their life.

At work and at home alike, Amun enjoys organisation. They are keen to ensure that everything runs smoothly during social or business occasions and commit themselves accordingly. Those born in this sign like to feel secure in their surroundings, so Amun always looks the part. They are, however, uneasy standing out in a crowd, so generally adopt a conservative appearance.

Amun will take a leading role in social activities. They are always ready to give advice and are often the best shoulder on which to cry. They tend to keep quiet about their own dilemmas, however, preferring to sort out their problems themselves. In this respect they are private people and are most likely to open up only to a very close friend or member of their family, should they need help.

Amun is generally a brave and courageous individual, in command of most situations. They usually avoid from the outset circumstances where they might have trouble. They are confident and consistent, and their response to most problems is calm, controlled and effective. It is often difficult to tell what Amun is thinking or, more importantly, how they are feeling. Unless angered, Amuns keep their emotions very much under control. But if pushed too far, they may explode in temper, which is likely to shock those who thought they were a quiet, contained type.

Amun undertakes most activities in a precise and methodical way. A creature of regular habits, Amun rarely surprises people with uncharacteristic behaviour. Although they may be somewhat predictable, they are good-humoured and excellent conversationalists. With friends and romantic partners, they are always considerate and polite.

Amun is not the type to make large numbers of casual acquaintances, preferring instead a small circle of close friends. They can be disturbed by company not of their choosing, and often prefer to socialise with their own friends rather than those of their partner. For this reason, partners of Amun people might sometimes find themselves somewhat isolated.

Amun keeps a strict account of their money and economises whenever possible. Despite this trait, they're the type who like to drive a luxury car, or own the best technological gadgets, appliances and home furnishings that they can afford – status symbols are particularly important to Amun.

The Amun Parent

Home life means a great deal to Amun, and family roots run deep. Amuns are one of the most caring signs when it comes to the welfare of their children, although emotionally they may be somewhat restrained. They will encourage their young in their schoolwork but may be unresponsive to their personal problems. Typically, Amuns believe that others will be as strong (or reserved) as they are, and so tend to lack sympathy if their children face an emotional crisis. 'Just forget about it,' might be an easy solution for Amun, but they tend to be unaware that their offspring might not feel the same and would prefer to talk about their problems and have some support. However, Amuns always make certain that their children are well-dressed, fed and cared for, no matter what personal sacrifices it might be necessary to make.

The Amun Child

From a very early age, the Amun child will be a responsive and eager learner. Amun children like to know the reason – the full reason – for everything. They are seldom put off with a half answer and often become quite obsessed with a subject and devote a lot of time to exploring it. They work diligently at school and usually do well in class. There are seldom bad reports for the Amun child. They are keen to succeed in sports and often become team captains in such activities.

Amuns prefer routine and dislike change. A new school or having to move home can upset the young Amun considerably. Providing that their surroundings remain consistent, the Amun child is usually easy to please.

Amun has a constructive attitude to life and few Amun children will deliberately cause trouble or be destructive. They are particularly polite to adults but there is a tendency for the Amun child to be overbearing with other children. They are seldom bullies, although they usually insist on taking the lead with their friends.

The Amun Friend

Amuns are peace-loving and amiable, wishing to live in harmony with their associates and neighbours. Few Amuns are responsible for causing trouble of any kind. When annoyed, however, they have quite a temper. Beware of trying the patience of Amun. Once hurt or angered, Amun is slow to forgive and will never forget. They make loyal and supportive friends, but fearsome enemies.

Amuns are somewhat possessive in relationships and friendships alike. They choose their acquaintances carefully, making sure they mix with others who share their beliefs and sentiments. Accordingly, there are seldom conflicts of interest. However, if one of their friends should change their attitudes or find others with whom to spend more time, Amun may feel personally insulted. Amuns make devoted friends but are uneasy about casual acquaintances of any kind.

The Amun Partner

Despite outward appearances, which are often reserved, Amun people are passionate and uninhibited lovers, although romantic sentiment is not a natural Amun trait. Keen to establish order and routine in their lives, they often settle down young. This can sometimes lead to hasty decisions. In fact, forging romantic relationships is about the only time in Amun's life when they do not think long and hard about a commitment. If the right partner is found, Amun will do everything they can to ensure that the partnership succeeds.

Amun enjoys flattery and admiration, particularly from prospective romantic partners. This sometimes results in misguided assumptions. The fact that Amuns are inclined to innocent flirtation can lead their partners to believe that they are being unfaithful. This is seldom true of Amun: they are usually the most loyal partners of any sign. Those born in this phase are deeply hurt when a relationship fails. Break-ups demoralise Amun considerably and all aspects of their lives may suffer as a result. When a relationship ends, Amun sees it as a personal failure. Amuns have considerable difficulty coping with turmoil or coming to terms with change.

Amun and Other Signs

Affinity Signs

SEKHMET: Industrious and optimistic Sekhmet is admired by Amun. Both signs share the ability to devote themselves consistently to a single objective or goal.

THE SPHINX: The Sphinx is the type that Amun often admires the most. Their ability to make something out of nothing, together with their keen financial instinct, is greatly respected by Amun.

WADJET: Wadjet is a sign of wisdom and those born in this phase are particularly creative concerning practical endeavours. Amun is a materialist and so the two signs complement one another. They lead similar social lives, and close friendships and attachments are common.

Incompatible Signs

SHU: Shu is far too sensitive and emotional for Amun, while Amun is too overbearing for Shu. The two signs have little in common, and their outlooks on life differ considerably.

THOTH and THE PHOENIX: Amun likes consistency. Both these signs are too erratic by far.

HATHOR: Hathor hates being controlled, whereas Amuns love being in control. This combination does not work well.

Compatibility with Other Signs

OSIRIS: Amun and Osiris often have many interests in common. However, Osiris hates being told what to do. Amun is sometimes too authoritative for Osiris's liking.

HORUS: Horus is a particularly affectionate sign, and Amun tends to distrust open displays of affection. Amun, however, can sometimes provide an emotional balance for Horus.

ANUBIS: Anubis and Amun mix well socially as both are polite and confident types. When working together, however, there can be clashes of interest. In partnerships there may be problems as both are exceptionally stubborn.

AMUN: Amuns generally get on great with other Amuns, as they all love order and consistency in their lives. However, this isn't always the case and occasionally Amuns might clash, as both struggle for control. Close partnerships are probably the most difficult relationships for them to handle.

ISIS: Amun admires the resourceful Isis, but Isis often finds Amun far too conventional in their approach to life.

Trends and Influences Through the Year

Over the course of the year Amun can expect the following influences to affect their lives during the separate Egyptian sign-phases:

THOTH August 29 – September 27:
This is a phase of movement, change and versatility. Amun dislikes having to alter direction, but it's likely they'll be forced to modify a strategy, whether it's a work or domestic situation. Amun should beware of expecting everything to remain the same. Any Amun considering a change of work or location may find it profitable to start their search at this time.

HORUS September 28 – October 27:
During the phase of Horus, Amun should make time for relaxation. Sport and other leisure-time activities are favourably placed, and vacations taken during this time can be especially fulfilling for Amun.

WADJET October 28 – November 26:
The wise Serpent brings contemplation to Amun. At this time of the year Amun may become somewhat withdrawn in social circumstances. Relationships, particularly with colleagues or close friends, may suffer.

SEKHMET November 27 – December 26:
Domestic matters may require much of Amun's attention. They should try to divide their time equally between work, rest and play. Unusual occurrences around the end of this phase may bring a radical change in everyday affairs. This is often a favourable time for love, romance and affairs of the heart.

THE SPHINX December 27 – January 25:
The Sphinx phase is often a time of conundrum, when complex circumstances are likely to confront Amun. Friends, relatives or work colleagues will be particularly helpful and may even provide solutions to longstanding problems Amun has been unable to resolve. The Sphinx acts as the message-bearer for Amun. Surprising news can be expected around the end of this phase.

SHU January 26 – February 24:
Airy Shu and earthy Amun are signs that are often worlds apart. This period is usually uneventful, and with little change.

ISIS February 25 – March 26:
During this phase, it's not uncommon for Amun to act completely out of character. Based simply on intuition or instinct, Amun may make an inspired decision. A new enterprise or relationship forged during this period is likely to bring considerable reward.

OSIRIS March 27 – April 25:
This may be a time of considerable frustration for Amun. Osiris is a sign of intangibility and Amun dislikes anything they

cannot pin down. In the Osiris phase, Amuns may find it particularly difficult to get to grips with the circumstances surrounding them.

AMUN April 26 – May 25:
Amun should be careful during their own phase. They should give and take a little more and accept that sometimes things don't go to plan. Others have their own ideas that Amun should take into consideration. If Amun lets circumstances be as they are, this can be an extremely favourable time for romance.

HATHOR May 26 – June 24:
This is a phase of financial reward for many Amuns. Good news, especially concerning monetary matters, is to be expected. Amun is not a gambler by nature, but a risk taken during this period is likely to be rewarded.

THE PHOENIX June 25 – July 24:
Many Amuns find the renewing Phoenix brings them fresh opportunities, particularly of a financial or business nature. Affairs of the heart may be problematic, however, due to a tendency by Amun to apply themselves too much to material matters.

ANUBIS July 25 – August 28:
Anubis is Amun's most favourable phase for romance and adventure. They seldom let themselves get carried away by emotion, but might find they have little choice during this period. Any Amun looking for a new love in their life may be pleasantly surprised during this phase.

Hathor

May 26 – June 24

Thou art the Mistress of Jubilation, the Queen of the Dance, the Mistress of Music, the Lady of the Choral Dance, the Mistress of Inebriety Without End.

From an ancient Hymn to Hathor.

Usually, the goddess Hathor was depicted in human form, wearing on her head the sun-disc flanked by a cow's horns, but she was sometimes portrayed in the form of a white cow. Her name in Ancient Egyptian was Het-Hert, which meant 'mansion of Horus' – and in some remaining records Horus is named as her consort.

Hathor was both a goddess of the land and of the sky, and had strong associations with love, music and dancing. As such, her phase is influenced by her grace and charm. One of the most popular goddesses, worshipped by both royalty and common people alike, Hathor was the personification of feminine love and motherhood, including assisting women in childbirth. She was also a goddess of the afterlife, greeting the newly-dead into their new existence with motherly love, offering food and drink. She also has strong associations with the cat-headed goddess, Bast, sharing some of her attributes, and occasionally was portrayed with the head of a lioness: there was a legend which told of her turning into the fierce goddess Sekhmet, to punish humanity when it had offended the sun god Ra.

Generally possessing great artistic flair, those born in Hathor's phase do not accept art for its own sake, seeking instead practical applications for their creations. Hathors may get carried away with enthusiasm, but they work best if they control and direct their creativity. Once they discover a balance between the down-to-earth and the imaginative, those born in this sign are free to accomplish outstanding achievements. Many Hathors have both spiritual and material aspirations. It is as though their feet are in two different worlds. Although they are highly imaginative, most Hathors are realists and few are content to live in a world of make-believe. Their intuitive decisions are often implemented with firm, rational logic.

If circumstances are working in their favour, Hathors can be outgoing and extrovert. Conversely, if they do not have the right support or encouragement they are prone to become shy and retiring. Generally, they enjoy being the centre of attention. Even the shy Hathor, who spends much of their time in seclusion, will find that their work ensures their fame.

The strongest motivation for Hathor is to be able to enjoy life to the full. They have the knack of living well, even if they have little money. Those born in this sign are experts at obtaining the best from most situations. Hathors have a generous nature and gain much contentment from helping others. If those around Hathor are happy, so are they.

Positive Qualities

Blessed with natural charm, Hathors are expressive and theatrical, with easily stimulated emotions. They have tremendous enthusiasm for new ideas, possessing an original way of thinking, a quick intellect and a good memory. Hathor has the capacity to learn easily. They have a romantic temperament and great love of travel and adventure. Neat and tidy, Hathor takes pride in their personal appearance.

Negative Traits

Impatience and intolerance often result in considerable frustration, and difficulties arise mainly through restlessness. For those born in this sign there is a tendency to fly to extremes, and irritability can strain relationships. Hathors have strong likes and dislikes, and their emotions are easily aroused. They are often impulsive, and extravagance is sometimes a problem. Envy is a Hathor trait, and jealousy needs to be controlled.

Appearance

The typical Hathor has sensitive features with large, expressive (though sometimes sorrowful) eyes. Although alert and active, most Hathors are graceful in their movements. Hathors are naturally sensual and are often charming and sophisticated. The facial features are particularly expressive.

Health

Many Hathors have problems with their feet, and breaking in new shoes can be agony for them. They are particularly vulnerable to colds and flu, after which they can suffer from lingering coughs. Bronchitis and other chest complaints are common for Hathors. On the positive side, few Hathors suffer from digestive complaints; ulcers are rare for them.

Optimising Hathor Attributes

Hathors find it difficult to run their lives along simple, well-organised lines. They often find themselves in difficult predicaments, usually due to good intentions and a tendency to expect others to act as considerately as they do themselves. Although generous, Hathor has a self-indulgent streak. If life is not full of variety and stimulation, they soon grow bored. They may forget their obligations and move on to new endeavours. Hathors also lack willpower, needing the moral support of others to achieve success. They are especially sensitive to adverse opinion and may admit defeat simply because someone else has told them that something will fail. Although they are strongly individualistic, they are anything but loners. Hathors need the encouragement of friends and associates. They are prone to stagnation and misery if left without support. Although they might find it difficult, Hathors should try to have more faith in themselves.

Suitable Occupations

Intuition, imagination and versatility are Hathor qualities, and many born in this sign achieve the best results once they have discovered an application for these traits. Ideal professions for Hathors are those offering scope for their artistic talents. Hathor is one of the most imaginative signs and can excel in all branches of the arts. The most outgoing will be drawn to dance, music and acting. Their creativity and keen eye for artistic detail also ensures they can be very successful in the fields of beauty therapy, hairdressing and as stylists and designers. The more retiring Hathor may concentrate on painting, writing or sculpture, which allows them to be apart from others for much of their time. Their much-needed appreciation comes via the success of their work.

Most Hathors commit themselves to the good of others, so social work and health care are also suitable occupations. Hathors make excellent child minders or carers for the sick or elderly. Another appropriate career is to become involved in youth schemes and other forms of community work.

The Hathor at Work

Hathor can be most misleading. A shy Hathor will be strong and motivated in times of crisis, whereas the tougher Hathor can be a real softie inside. Work colleagues are often surprised by Hathor, who suddenly displays abilities or talents they least expected. It is a mistake for any prospective employer to readily categorise Hathor, especially during an interview. What you see is not all you get with the self-conscious Hathor. Hathors may not handle their own affairs with the thrift of some signs, but when it comes to business matters they have a good head for profit.

The Hathor Personality

Hathors are by nature cool, calm and collected people, but with an inner vigour. They are usually the centre of attention. They are great conversationalists and eager listeners; their company is much appreciated by all. Even the shy Hathor is an entertaining companion when apart from the crowd – they too enjoy attention as much as their more outgoing counterpart.

Always popular within their social scene, others might sometimes resent the attention Hathors receive. In fact, it's not unusual for Hathors to find themselves the focus of other people's envy, who might wish they possessed some of Hathor's effortless popularity and grace. This can occasionally lead to Hathor having trouble making close friends, as envy within friendships can lead to conflict too often for Hathor's liking.

Hathors are not loud or fiery conversationalists, and their sense of humour often leaves something to be desired, but this is offset by their smooth-talking charm. Few Hathors are boisterous or vulgar and have innate refinement.

Those born in this sign are not drawn to extreme physical activities – they would rather do Yoga or Tai Chi than take part in a rigorous sporting activity. If they are involved in sport, this is likely to be in a leadership or organising capacity rather than one of the team. Many Hathors have an interest in politics, where their skill with language can be exercised to the full.

Hathor is naturally a neat and tidy person, although they are far more concerned with their personal appearance than with their environment. It can come as a complete shock for a first-time visitor to a Hathor's home – their personal living space might be nowhere near as orderly as you'd expect.

With romantic partners, Hathor will be thoughtful and accommodating. They treat their lovers well and with consideration, and often shower them with gifts.

The Hathor Parent

Many Hathors enjoy strong family ties. The more people to love and be loved by, the happier they are. In many ways, Hathor parents may be a little too lax with their children. They strongly disapprove of punishment of any kind, preferring instead to reward their children for success rather than scold them for failure. Hathors are among the best at comforting a child who has failed an examination, is having trouble at school, or is in distress of any kind. Many Hathors tend to spoil their children.

The Hathor Child

Often a gentle, loving child, the sensitive Hathor needs much encouragement to face the harder realities of life. They are the first to succumb to tears and really feel the blows of life more than other children. Hathors are dreamers, and are prone to have invisible childhood friends, or will regularly talk to themselves. Many will spend hours playing alone.

Hathor children mature later than those of other signs.

Sometimes this means that they are bullied or badgered by older children. In their teens, however, they quickly learn to stand up for themselves. Hathors are not aggressive by nature, and generally abhor physical violence. When necessary, however, they are quite prepared to meet like with like.

Hathor children are especially creative, and many excel in the arts. The sciences, however, seldom appeal to the Hathor child. Teachers might complain about their performance in subjects like mathematics, chemistry or physics. Few children born in this sign pay much attention to lessons in which they have absolutely no interest.

The Hathor Friend

There is a mercurial quality to Hathor that often confuses friends. Unconsciously, Hathors can adopt the attitudes, habits and mannerisms of those with whom they are closely associated. This is one reason that Hathors are so popular – they can be all things to all people.

Although Hathors enjoy flattery and attention, most retain a genuine modesty regarding their work. Indeed, some find it hard to accept praise for their professional achievements. This can puzzle Hathor's friends, who may wonder if they have somehow offended them with a heart-felt compliment.

Hathor modesty is genuine, although some of their reactions are not. They are natural actors, not above feigning enthusiasm for something in which they have no real interest. Hathor may seem riveted by your conversation, when all the time they are bored stiff. Hathors are especially polite and hate to offend. They avoid, however, going through a tedious experience twice.

The Hathor Partner

The personal life of Hathor would provide rich material for the romantic novelist. Falling in and out of love is a regular habit for those born in this sign. Hathors share an idealistic, if not unrealistic, attitude to romance. Even if a relationship ends in disaster, Hathor remains eternally optimistic about future affairs. They seem to believe that love is exactly as it is in the movies. If a relationship fails to blossom, they are often deeply hurt, and usually blame themselves. Hathors, however, are not possessive lovers and few will continue to throw unwanted attentions in an ex-partner's direction.

Hathors enjoy romance to the extent that serious commitments seldom come early. When they eventually do settle down, it is generally Hathor's partner who takes the lead. Hathor expects their partners to pull their weight with domestic chores, and in some cases tend to heap their significant other with most of the household jobs. Hathors are adept at persuading their partner to do exactly what they want – at precisely the right moment they can turn on the tears or the charm.

Though vulnerable to passing infatuation, Hathor is capable of considerable loyalty. If love begins to fade, however, Hathor fidelity will soon follow suit. Hathor hates to hurt another's feelings, and sometimes they find it difficult to terminate one affair before another begins.

Hathor and Other Signs

Affinity Signs

THOTH: Hathor particularly enjoys the company of Thoth. Hathor's romanticism is often inspired by Thoth's adventurous spirit.

THE PHOENIX: Hathor likes the company of the Phoenix. Both have a romantic temperament that can inspire each other to achieve great success.

ANUBIS: Anubis and Hathor are particularly compatible signs, especially concerning romantic affiliations. They share common interests, although their personalities are sufficiently different not to clash.

ISIS: Hathors are often attracted to unconventional Isis, while Isis moves towards those with imagination. These signs are most compatible, and many successful relationships and working partnerships result.

Incompatible Signs

AMUN: Hathor hates being controlled, while Amuns love being in control.

HATHOR: Hathor does not find it easy to mix well with others similar to themselves. Two Hathors may find that they are in constant competition with one another.

OSIRIS: Hathor is too sentimental for Osiris. Hathor seeks close relationships, and has a need for firm, emotional commitments. Osiris feels too restricted by such demands.

Compatibility with Other Signs

HORUS: Horus and Hathor both allow their imaginations a free reign. Consequently, the two signs may behave somewhat irresponsibly when together.

WADJET: Hathor finds the learned Wadjet of considerable interest. They may, however, distrust Wadjet's cool, laid-back approach to life.

SEKHMET: Relationships between Hathors and Sekhmets are particularly volatile. They may adore one another, sharing a love of adventure, travel and excitement. When together, however, both can find their emotions too readily stimulated and arguments may result. These signs often share a love/hate relationship.

THE SPHINX: Hathors generally admire the clever Sphinx, whereas Sphinxes often find the romantic Hathor a stimulating companion.

SHU: Shus and Hathors both share an interest in the exotic and unusual aspects of life. Close friendships and relationships are possible, although partnership between these two signs can sometimes suffer due to a lack of practical considerations.

Trends and Influences Through the Year

Over the course of the year Hathor can expect the following influences to affect their lives during the separate Egyptian sign-phases:

THOTH August 29 – September 27:
This phase can be a time of success, especially in business matters. However, Hathors should avoid locking horns with the influences of this phase. They should let things be as they are, rather than how they would wish them to be.

HORUS September 28 – October 27:
This is the best time of year for Hathor to take a vacation. Weekends away can be particularly romantic. Business matters or complex decisions concerning domestic life are best left until Hathor has their feet more firmly on the ground.

WADJET October 28 – November 26:
Wadjet acts as a message-bearer for Hathor. News received during the early days of this phase can result in a new outlook on life. This is also a time well-aspected for financial and monetary matters.

SEKHMET November 27 – December 26:
At no other time of the year is Hathor more likely to lose patience than during the phase of Sekhmet. Problems in relationships or with close friends or colleagues may occur because of Hathor irritability.

THE SPHINX December 27 – January 25:
For Hathor, this phase is a time of learning. Hathors involved in academic pursuits will find this a particularly fruitful time of the year. Hathors generally find that solutions to problems will present themselves. Others should respect Hathor's point of view during the phase of the Sphinx – it is often wise, inspired and deeply intuitive.

SHU January 26 – February 24:
If there is a lurking problem in Hathor's life, this is the time of year when it is most likely to erupt. If there are difficulties in relationships, with friends or at work, they are likely to hit a crisis point. Should a situation end or change, this is a fortuitous time to act.

ISIS February 25 – March 26:
Isis's phase is especially linked to financial matters as far as Hathor is concerned. An unexpected windfall is possible. Any new enterprise initiated during this time is likely to reap rewards.

OSIRIS March 27 – April 25:
Hathors will often find that others rely on them during this phase. Most Hathors like attention and are helpful by nature. However, they may find that they are restricted by the constant demands of others.

AMUN April 26 – May 25:
Amun is a sign of authority. Many Hathors distrust authority and especially hate being ordered around. This is a phase

during which Hathor may find greatest difficulty. Someone close to them could attempt to persuade them to act against their wishes. Hathor should stand firm yet avoid becoming entangled in arguments and quarrels.

HATHOR May 26 – June 24:
During the phase of their own sign Hathors are in their imaginative element. Innovative ideas occur to them constantly, and fresh possibilities are eagerly grasped. This is a particularly favourable time for anything to do with music or the arts.

THE PHOENIX June 25 – July 24:
In legend, the Phoenix continually rose from the ashes. This phase is a time for new opportunities for Hathor. Something long-awaited may come to fruition. New friendships or relationships are possible. Sport and leisure activities, even games of chance, are favourable for Hathor at this time.

ANUBIS July 25 – August 28:
The imaginative and adventurous Hathor is well-placed for romance during the phase of Anubis. An existing partnership is likely to be enhanced by new prospects, particularly concerning domestic matters and the home. Any Hathor on the lookout for a new partner may be pleasantly surprised. New acquaintances and friendships are possible.

The Phoenix

June 25 – July 24

I have gone forth as a Phoenix, Lord of Jubilees, risen and shining.
From a tomb inscription in the Valley of the Kings.

The sacred firebird, known to the Ancient Egyptians as the 'Benu', was a symbol of the sun, life and rebirth. In legend, this exotic bird made its nest of spices, and when the sun's rays set it alight the Phoenix was burned to cinders. A few days later, a new Phoenix was born, rising majestically from the ashes of the old. It's possible that the Benu was the inspiration for the later Greek representation of the phoenix.

In appearance, the Benu resembled a heron, its head adorned with the Atef crown, worn also by Osiris. It was believed to be instrumental in the creation of the earth in several different Egyptian creation myths. One of its epithets is 'He Who Came into Being by Himself', meaning that it was spontaneously created rather than born like any other creature. The Benu is a symbol of resilience and hope, since it rises anew from its own death. It can be seen as an icon of endless possibilities.

The main characteristic of those born in the sign of the Phoenix is the ability to create opportunities. They are optimistic in the extreme, seldom accepting any situation as hopeless. Usually able to find some good even in their worst enemies, the Phoenix is remarkably resilient. They have a close affinity with nature and are often conservationists and vegetarians or vegans.

Travel has enormous appeal for the Phoenix, who tends to be attracted to secluded spots. They prefer hot climates – winter holidays in a snowy landscape are not for them. Born in a phase for which the symbol is a creature of fire, the Phoenix dislikes the cold intensely. However, they can function well in even the worst of heat waves, rushing around busily while others are sweltering. Hot or spicy foods are also a favourite for the Phoenix. Preferring to be active, sedentary occupations such as reading or watching TV are not high on the Phoenix list of priorities. The exceptions are sports or game shows, which the Phoenix may follow avidly.

The Phoenix has tremendous vitality. Life is an adventure for them, although a craving for excitement may lead to difficult situations. Always eager for new experiences, and ready to rise to the challenge, the Phoenix's life is full of surprises. They are often so keen to fill their lives with excitement that sometimes they neglect the smaller and more practical matters. Phoenixes are often impatient with waiting for opportunities to arise; they prefer to create their own. In fact, they consider it their personal responsibility to seek out new and interesting possibilities.

Positive Qualities

Resilient, optimistic and determined, the Phoenix has an inventive and adaptable personality. They are industrious and highly active, and are able to find new uses for the most unlikely things. The Phoenix has a conscientious attitude to work and is rarely lazy or the type to cut corners. They also have a strong tendency to champion the plight of people less fortunate than themselves and are able to inspire confidence and enthusiasm in others.

Negative Traits

The Phoenix has a stubborn streak. They prefer to do things their own way – even when they know they are wrong. Often a dreamer, the Phoenix might refuse to face reality when problems occur. They can spend too much time on failed endeavours, when it would be better for them to move on to something else. The Phoenix is often headstrong and occasionally egotistical.

Appearance

Those born in this sign often have a determined appearance. Their intense eyes are extremely attractive to potential romantic partners. The Phoenix's nose is usually sharp, although the chin tends to be round. Weight is seldom a problem: an abundance of nervous energy generally keeps the Phoenix slim and agile. Some have a weathered or even rugged appearance, often due to regular outdoor activities. Many born in this sign have a streak of mischief in them.

Health

The Phoenix usually enjoys good health, although skin complaints can be a problem. More often than not, this is the result of stress. Diet is seldom a cause of concern. They can eat what they like without putting on too much weight, as the typical Phoenix has a high metabolism, plus the fact they generally have an active lifestyle. They might experience back problems in later life, owing to a tendency to stoop. The Phoenix is a symbol of vitality and those born in this phase are usually fit and trim.

Optimising Phoenix Attributes

Once Phoenixes have made up their minds, they are firm in their convictions. The Phoenix, however, is a sign of action rather than words, and handling a skilled debate is something they might find hard. When faced with opposition, the Phoenix generally loses patience, brushing off adverse opinion with an exasperated shrug. Few Phoenixes spend time consulting with others and are apt to jump to conclusions far too quickly. They sometimes lack sound judgement, although they more than compensate for this through an abundance of willpower. Most problems the Phoenix encounters arise from an inability to see things from someone else's point of view. Although they are sympathetic to those in obvious distress, they are usually so wrapped up in their own affairs that they take little interest in the opinions of others. Phoenixes should listen to those around them before arriving at conclusions.

Suitable Occupations

With an adventurous temperament, the Phoenix is especially suited for hazardous occupations. They are generally most successful when self-employed, as long as they have someone to keep the accounts for them. Few Phoenixes work well with money, and for this reason a career in finance would not be an optimal choice. Phoenix enthusiasm is contagious, and a career in sales or promotional work can be highly successful. Technically gifted, those born in this sign make excellent mechanics and engineers.

The Phoenix at Work

Happiest when working alone, the Phoenix is not at their best in a business partnership. In any working environment, if colleagues are prepared to let the Phoenix do things their own way, positive results often follow. Phoenixes make tough but fair employers, although they might drive their employees a little too hard. As an employee, the Phoenix has optimism, which is always a valuable contribution to any workforce. Sometimes, however, their optimism may prove frustrating, particularly if an enterprise is an obvious failure. The Phoenix just doesn't know when to quit.

The Phoenix Personality

While making great successes of their careers, the Phoenix is equally happy running a home, and is also more than capable of doing both at the same time excellently. They seem to find time in their lives for everything, where others might feel there's never enough. The capacity to multi-task with apparent effortlessness is helped by the Phoenix's abundance of energy.

Phoenixes will speak their minds frankly, always making their motives and objectives clear. Most signs know where they stand with the Phoenix. Tact is not a Phoenix attribute, however, and those of this sign tend to be forthright and outspoken. They seldom lose their temper, although they often become irritable if someone fails to understand their requirements. Phoenixes sometimes say more than is wise and find it difficult to apologise if they have offended without meaning to. Their usual form of apology is to make up for it in some way without ever actually saying they are sorry.

The Phoenix is more accident prone than other signs, often due to haste rather than carelessness. Although they are often preoccupied with the safety of others, they tend to disregard such precautions themselves. The Phoenix is skilled at manual tasks and is often so good at mending and installing things in the household, they seldom need to call in an expert, but it's no surprise to their families if they incur small injuries while doing such work.

Wildly enthusiastic about whoever or whatever is the focus of their attention, the Phoenix seems oblivious to anyone or anything else. It's virtually impossible to drag them away from anything in which they're involved, which can be annoying for friends and family who are waiting for them to do something else. However, the Phoenix hates to be kept waiting themselves. They are the first to lose patience when someone is late.

The Phoenix Parent

Phoenix parents usually expect their children to share their own interests and are often disappointed in this respect. They look after their children well but sometimes expect too much of them. They are rather too eager to tell them how to run their lives. Phoenix parents are not strict or overbearing by nature – they simply want their children to be like them. Phoenixes are usually concerned parents and offer their children considerable encouragement.

The Phoenix Child

In legend, the Phoenix was reborn in the heart of the desert. Like the firebird, Phoenix children are happy to spend time in seclusion. They are certainly not shy or reclusive: they are simply content to play alone. The Phoenix child can be a handful for parents and teachers alike. From infancy, the Phoenix makes it very clear they have a will of their own. Boisterous in play, they may be given to tantrums if they fail to get their own way. They are at their best when given liberty to think and act for themselves.

The competitive Phoenix spirit emerges in childhood, and most children born in this sign are keen to do well. Although many are good at sport, few succeed in team events. Individual events are best for them and they often excel at athletics or swimming. Phoenix children are not particularly good at taking care of their possessions, and a careless streak can result in many a broken toy. In childhood arguments, the Phoenix is unafraid to tackle a child older or bigger than themselves. Sometimes this can lead to brawls.

The Phoenix Friend

The Phoenix is one of the most robust of signs and those born in this phase have resilient personalities. They will not let the opinions of others deter or influence their actions, and they will completely ignore sneers or cruel remarks if something has failed.

Courageous by nature, the Phoenix is always ready to take risks for their friends. The Phoenix is good in a crisis and is usually the first to suggest a solution. Even if something seems hopeless, the Phoenix does not give up hope and inspires other to keep things calm and positive. In times of peril, the Phoenix will endanger themselves for the good of others, and in war they are often those decorated for feats of heroism.

Although they see the best in most people, Phoenixes dislike arrogance and despise aggression. They are kind and sympathetic to those who are shy or in distress; it is often the Phoenix who comes to the aid of those in trouble. Phoenixes make excellent companions for anyone prepared to take a back seat now and again. They are never boring to be around, but their need for occasional solitude can sometimes be taken the wrong way.

The Phoenix Partner

The Phoenix is seldom jealous. If their partner appears interested in someone else, they usually know precisely what to do about it. If they fail to resolve a relationship conflict, their response is generally to feel that their partner is not worth the effort. They expect their partners to work at the relationship – nourish it – and if they should fail to do so, the Phoenix will soon look elsewhere. In love, like in most areas of their lives, if something is not working out they are inclined to make a clean break and then quickly start again.

Not particularly sensual in love, the Phoenix may appear restrained in a relationship. However, they are kind and generous. The Phoenix may be a passionate lover, but are not the type for romantic small talk, which they'll most likely view as shallow and meaningless.

Because of their impetuous nature, the Phoenix can fall in love at first sight. They seldom dwell too long on any decision. Actions speak louder than words for the lover born in this sign, and many rush too readily into commitment. As long as the choice is right, however, relationships can be long-lasting.

Phoenixes make ideal partners as they hate domestic strife. They would rather give way to their partner's demands than create a fuss. There is usually too much else on their minds for them to become entangled in a quarrel. To them, conflict is simply a waste of time.

The Phoenix and Other Signs

Affinity Signs

SHU: The Phoenix gets on best with those who are less active than they are. Many born in the Shu sign are calm and serene – at least outwardly. Accordingly, they can exert a positive influence on the Phoenix's impulsive nature.

ISIS: Like the mythical bird, those born in the Phoenix phase will find themselves attracted to the exotic or unusual. Isis is perhaps the most intriguing of signs, and their idiosyncratic style is irresistible to the Phoenix.

THOTH: Thoth is a mood-swinger and their behaviour can be erratic. Unlike many signs, the Phoenix is almost impervious to the emotional swings of others. As both the Phoenix and Thoth need their own space, they make excellent partners and long-lasting relationships are possible.

HATHOR: The Phoenix particularly likes the company of Hathor. They have a romantic temperament that the Phoenix finds inspiring.

Incompatible Signs

HORUS: This is potentially the most problematic sign for the Phoenix. They can recover from failure and setbacks, but Horus finds this hard. Both signs are adventurous, but when the Phoenix burns to ashes it rises again. The two signs get on great to begin with, but should problems occur the Phoenix cannot understand Horus's inability to cope.

AMUN and WADJET: Wadjet and Amun are generally types with whom the Phoenix finds greatest difficulty. Both leadership signs, they enjoy taking charge far too much for Phoenix's liking.

Compatibility with Other Signs

OSIRIS: The Phoenix and Osiris often work well together, although in relationships the Phoenix usually seeks consistency generally lacking in Osiris's life.

SEKHMET: Both Sekhmet and the Phoenix are signs of extreme optimism, and the two get on like a house on fire; after all, they are both creatures of fire. Unfortunately, they both need the restraining elements of other signs. Together, the Phoenix and Sekhmet can find themselves in bad situations that are difficult to solve.

THE PHOENIX: Two Phoenixes work well together but, like two Sekhmets, problems can arise through too little care or planning.

ANUBIS: Phoenixes find Anubis too pragmatic. These signs seldom mix well as close companions, although on a superficial level there are few problems.

THE SPHINX: The Phoenix dislike of financial matters is well compensated for by the Sphinx. The Sphinx is both conservative and thrifty in their approach to most endeavours, and the Phoenix respects such attributes in others.

Trends and Influences Through the Year

Over the course of the year the Phoenix can expect the following influences to affect their lives during the separate Egyptian sign-phases:

THOTH August 29 – September 27:
Thoth brings imaginative and fresh ideas to the Phoenix mind. New notions conceived during this phase are likely to be well-founded. During this phase, the Phoenix will make sound decisions.

HORUS September 28 – October 27:
The Phoenix should be more careful during this period than at any other time. Both Horus and the Phoenix are given to taking dangerous risks. Horus will face adversity with great courage, when perhaps retreat would be more sensible, while the Phoenix has little fear of failure. Combined, these influences are apt to leave the Phoenix wide open to rash decisions.

WADJET October 28 – November 26:
As a sign of wisdom, Wadjet balances Phoenix impetuosity. This can be an especially favourable period for complicated matters previously unresolved. Sporting activities are particularly favoured for the Phoenix at this time. As Wadjet is the message-bearer for the Phoenix, surprise news can also be expected during this phase.

SEKHMET November 27 – December 26:
Both the Phoenix and Sekhmet are creatures of fire. During this phase, Phoenix imagination will be at its most effective. Most projects are likely to succeed due to the quick reactions of the Phoenix. Relationships or friendships may suffer, however, as the Phoenix may be particularly argumentative at this time.

THE SPHINX December 27 – January 25:
This phase can be a period of stagnation for the Phoenix. If things do not seem to be moving ahead as quickly as they hoped, matters should be given a little more time.

SHU January 26 – February 24:
Very often, the Phoenix will be in their element during a Shu phase. Normal practical restraints will be lifted by the influence of Shu, and the firebird is free to soar to new heights. Romantic, financial and leisure activities are all favourably placed. This is a time of good luck in matters of chance.

ISIS February 25 – March 26:
This phase favours influences from the past having positive bearing on the present. The Phoenix might have an unexpected meeting with an old acquaintance. This may open a completely new chapter in the Phoenix's life.

OSIRIS March 27 – April 25:
Romantic disappointments are possible, although it is a particularly favourable period for financial affairs. New opportunities often arise during this phase for the Phoenix, while long-standing projects may end. This is very much a time of change.

AMUN April 26 – May 25:
A combination of assertive Amun and the determined Phoenix is favourable for business matters. This is especially a time of good fortune in financial affairs. Conversely, it is not a particularly romantic period for the Phoenix. Difficulties in relationships are possible due to distractions and preoccupations.

HATHOR May 26 – June 24:
During this phase, the Phoenix should try to keep their imagination under control. There is a tendency to forge ahead

far too quickly. A cautious approach to most endeavours is advised. Any Phoenix seeking love or romance, however, may be pleasantly surprised at this time of the year.

THE PHOENIX June 25 – July 24:
In the phase of the Phoenix, those born under its sign will find it a favourable period for travel, change of location or employment. Good news, especially by mail, can be expected.

ANUBIS July 25 – August 28:
For the Phoenix, this phase can be a time of relative tranquillity. Few Phoenixes are quiet or reserved by nature, and impatience may result. Many Phoenixes will find themselves especially frustrated by humdrum, everyday events. This is a good time to take a break. Vacations and leisure activities are favourably placed.

Anubis

July 25 – August 28

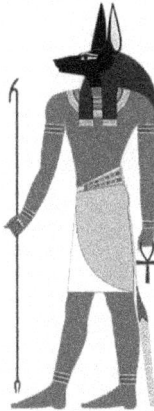

O Anubis, Lord of the hallowed land,
weigh my soul at the time of my crossing.
From the Egyptian Book of the Dead.

The jackal-headed god Anubis, known in Ancient Egypt as Anpu, was the guardian of the underworld and the judge of souls. He was also a deity of mummification and the afterlife. He presided over the ceremony of the 'Weighing of the Heart' in the underworld, when it was decided whether a newly-deceased person's soul was fit to enter the afterlife. His symbols were the flail and a funerary object originally known as Imiut fetish, which was a stuffed feline or bull skin attached to a pole and used during funeral rites. His consort was another funerary deity, the goddess Anput and his daughter was the serpent goddess, Kebechet, (Qeb-hwt), who was associated with embalming fluid, thereby keeping a body fresh and uncorrupted, so it remained viable for reanimation.

It's interesting how the jackal might have become an animal associated with the afterlife. It's thought this is similar to how Sekhmet, a goddess believed to cause disease, became associated with healing. Jackals were scavengers who frequented graveyards looking for carrion, so to the Egyptians it might have seemed obvious that these creatures would therefore be adept at guarding the dead – they must know so much about them! And perhaps they were drawn to cemeteries and tombs because it was their natural environment. Concerning their deities, the Ancient Egyptians often had a very practical view.

Anubis could be said to have knowledge others do not, since he knew the territory of the afterlife – not as a kingly god like Osiris, but as the usher who steered the ordinary people into their new existence. He was a judge but also a guide.

Those born in the sign of Anubis are usually creative and imaginative, yet retain a firm interest in practical affairs. They may be business people or artists, yet whichever profession they choose both attributes are brought into play. This is probably the most determined of all the signs. Anubis is self-assured in most situations, and a natural capacity to take control affords them much respect. Anubis has an air of authority but is quite prepared to work behind the scenes. To those born in this sign, it is the task that is important, not by whom or how it is achieved.

For Anubis everything has its place. There is a time for work, a time for rest and a time for play. They commit themselves fully to each but hate to mix the three. Anubis people will devote themselves exclusively to whatever they are doing. They enjoy routine and keep regular habits. Anubis has a marvellous capacity to work hard all day but, once they have finished for the evening, their minds are tuned exclusively to relaxation. Unless they have something specific to do, Anubis is content to sit for hours, watching television, reading a book or listening to music.

The Anubis is unafraid of failure or recrimination and is quite prepared to be disbelieved, even ridiculed, until their point is proven. Insults or sneers have little influence on Anubis, as they possess the confidence and self-assurance to believe they are right. Anubis people seldom commit themselves to any enterprise about which they are uncertain. Those born in this sign are prepared to persevere long and hard to achieve results.

Positive Qualities

Anubis people have a determined spirit with great capacity for creative thinking. They have sympathetic and hospitable personalities, and their spiritual aspirations are usually well-developed. Anubis has a generous nature and an idealistic attitude to life. The common good is usually a high priority for them, and they're prepared to make personal sacrifices to help those around them. Many have a philosophical attitude to life and most have faith that good will ultimately triumph.

Negative Traits

Relationships are sometimes made difficult by an obstinate spirit. There is a marked tendency to disregard the attitudes of others or offend without intent. Anubis needs to consider every angle of a problem, which so often leads to too much preparation and not enough action. Frequently, Anubis people fail to seize opportunities offered them on a plate.

Appearance

The Anubis gaze is direct and benevolent. They have a habit of nodding knowingly when listening and adopt an understanding smile – even when they disagree completely with what they hear. Anubis people move with an air of confidence. They carry their heads high and walk with their backs straight. At rest, however, Anubis tends to sprawl.

Health

The Anubis ability to relax completely may result in weight problems. Few Anubis people are worriers, and those born in this sign are seldom concerned about their own well-being. Many are therefore inclined to ignore preventative medicine or disregard any tell-tale signs of illness. Ailments that are best tackled early may be left unattended by Anubis. This can lead to complications that might easily have been avoided.

Optimising Anubis Attributes

Anubis was the guardian of the underworld. Like their mythical counterpart, those born in this sign are protective by nature. Once something is theirs, they hate to give it up. Anubis people will adhere to a notion, or continue with an enterprise, even when it is outmoded or doomed to failure. They should take time to re-examine their circumstances and adjust their approach when necessary. As Anubis considers every factor before embarking on a venture, most endeavours are likely to succeed. Should failure result from unforeseen circumstances, however, Anubis is usually ill-prepared to deal with it. To avoid being left stranded, Anubis people should remember to keep a backup plan in reserve.

Suitable Occupations

Anubis people flourish in many trades and professions. As keen planners and organisers they fare particularly well in commerce. An artistic Anubis has tremendous insight into what is popular; advertising and the world of fashion employs many Anubis people in prominent positions. Anubis types are equally content to work behind the scenes. In the world of entertainment, for instance, as many Anubis people are found off-stage as in the public eye. Those who do perform before an audience usually do so in a unique and unusual way. Those in manual trades love to see an enterprise develop through every stage to completion. They are keen to witness the result of their contribution. Few Anubis people are comfortable in a closed working environment.

The Anubis at Work

Anubis makes a considerate employer, exercising authority without becoming demonstrative or overbearing. They are always concerned for the well-being of their staff and make certain that they are kept informed concerning all aspects of their work. Although Anubis people make excellent bosses, they are not the best of entrepreneurs. In management, Anubis lacks the ruthless streak sometimes necessary to make financially-sound decisions. Concern for their workforce is likely to preside over interests of sheer profit. As employees, Anubis people make a positive contribution to the workforce. They are, however, inclined to side with those in difficulty, and Anubis's willingness to defend an unpopular workmate can result in friction with colleagues.

The Anubis Personality

Anubis is the most composed of any sign. They are assured, debonair, calm and collected, although not arrogant or aloof. Panache comes naturally to them. Although they're not by nature overly flirtatious, they enjoy the attention of others. A certain intangible mystique turns many an eye in their direction. Anubis people are usually trendsetters rather than followers. They are certainly not conservative in style, although in their clothing they choose quality over variety, often preferring darker colours.

Those born in this phase are seldom loners, and most enjoy being part of a group. They like to stand out in a crowd. They are cannot stand bigotry and intolerance, and hate seeing others being oppressed or bullied. They are the first to offer support to those who are victims of aggression or cruelty.

In their careers, Anubis can be the most successful of signs. The mythical Anubis was a guardian, and those born in this phase have strong family ties. They are proud of their homes and of their family's achievements and like to provide for those they love. But they also like to keep their home environment apart from the rest of their lives. At work Anubises are fully dedicated to their tasks, and might come across as workaholics, but at home they forget about their work and become devoted, domesticated family types. They commit themselves to each aspect of their lives with equal enthusiasm but keep them entirely separate.

Anubis people are often collectors of mementoes and memorabilia. In particular, they enjoy keeping a record of their lives and are often keen photographers. They are also captivated by hobbies, and most have a pet interest to occupy their spare time. Anubises commit themselves equally to work, rest and play – but each has a set place and time. Beware of arriving at Anubis's home unannounced – they will be most put out if their routine is disturbed. Anubis needs adequate warning of anything that may disrupt their life or necessitate a change of plan.

The Anubis Parent

The Anubis parent is inclined to be overprotective of their children. They are worriers, who always want to know where their offspring are and what they're up to. Although this is an admirable quality for parents of younger children, when those offspring reach their teens it can be somewhat restricting for them, and conflicts are likely to arise. Parents of other signs may be prepared to let their teenage children stay over at friends or go to parties and get home late, but an Anubis parent is more likely to keep their offspring grounded or impose strict curfews.

Anubis is very proud of their children and is swift to stick up for them if there are disagreements with teachers. Conflicts are therefore a possibility with school authorities. Anubis parents can be blind to faults in their children and tend to react strongly if others dare to criticise their offspring. They want to shield them from life's traumas.

The Anubis Child

Most Anubis children are relaxed in adult company, which some may find disconcerting. They mature early and seldom act the fool. From a very early age, Anubis children exhibit a responsible and conscientious attitude to life. They work well in class but hate doing homework. Like their adult counterparts, they feel that once the working day has ended it is time to relax. Revising does not come easily, so examinations may suffer. If they enter higher education, however, the regulated Anubis life-style can prove extremely useful. Unlike some students who may skip lectures, Anubis will attend college conscientiously, as if they were already employed and paid to do a job.

The Anubis Friend

Loyalty is an Anubis virtue that remains undaunted in the face of crisis. Anubis people will be especially staunch on a friend's behalf. They are idealists, always ready to come to the aid of others. Anubis people handle criticism well and seldom take offence. Accordingly, they make easy-going friends, especially for those who are outspoken or temperamental. Excitability, erratic behaviour or changes of mood are easily taken in Anubis's stride. All Anubis asks of their friends is fairness and honesty. Anubis people seldom hold a grudge and are quick to forgive.

Those born in this phase do not show particularly sound judgement regarding those around them, however. They live as if in an ideal world and believe that others will act as considerately as they do. Therefore, many Anubis people suffer from disappointments in working and personal relationships.

A prime Anubis fault is their devotion to schedules. If Anubis's timetabled life is disturbed, they can be thrown into turmoil. You will not always know when the obliging Anubis is upset. They may agree with your plans to disrupt their routine, only to spend the rest of the day repeatedly looking at their watch.

The Anubis Partner

Anubis is affectionate and protective, although not romantic by nature. Those born in this sign look for home comforts in a relationship rather than romantic bliss. They seek life companions who are homely and consistent. They want devoted, domesticated partners, who are steady and reliable.

Anubis people throw themselves completely into their relationships and expect their partners to do the same. This, of course, will not always happen as they would like, particularly in the early days of dating. Such premature Anubis expectations are sometimes disturbing to those of other signs, who may need longer to make firm commitments. If Anubis was not so impatient to settle down, many a failed relationship might have developed quite differently. Anubis people should always remember that partners often need more time.

Anubis and Other Signs

Affinity Signs

THOTH: Anubis works very well with Thoth. Thoth imagination can develop Anubis's more practical ideas, and both have considerable creativity. The two signs also complement each other in business matters.

HATHOR: Anubis and Hathor are particularly compatible signs, especially concerning romantic affiliations. They share common interests, although their personalities are sufficiently different not to clash.

SHU: Anubis's strong family ties and protective instincts can make them ideal partners for Shus. Shus often look at life from a very different perspective to Anubis, and their romantic imagination usually aids Anubis's creativity.

OSIRIS: Anubis people are prepared to give others their own space – something Osiris desperately needs and therefore appreciates. Unlike some signs, Anubis is usually open about themselves, having no problem with Osiris inquisitiveness.

Incompatible Signs

ANUBIS: Anubis people often get on well with their own type in a platonic sense. However, romantic relationships may not go so well, as both have such high expectation of partners.

SEKHMET: Sekhmets and Anubis are both creative signs. However, the headstrong Anubis can often clash with the fiery temperament of Sekhmet. Neither is prepared to give way to the other.

THE SPHINX: The Sphinx and Anubis often experience a clash of interests and personalities. Sometimes they may even distrust one another.

ISIS: Isis can unnerve Anubis. Few Anubis people like ideas as unconventional as those born in the sign of Isis appear to display.

Compatibility with Other Signs

THE PHOENIX: Phoenixes find Anubis people too pragmatic. Although on a superficial level these two signs may tolerate one other, they seldom mix well as close companions.

AMUN: Anubises and Amuns mix well socially, as both are polite and confident signs. When working together, however, there can be clashes of interest. In partnerships, there may be problems as both signs are exceptionally stubborn.

HORUS: Anubis and Horus have few problems socially, although Horus is seldom prepared to make the sort of long-term commitments Anubis expects.

WADJET: Anubis people like to know precisely where they stand and so find Wadjet difficult to fathom.

Trends and Influences Through the Year

Over the course of the year Anubis can expect the following influences to affect their lives during the separate Egyptian sign-phases:

THOTH August 29 – September 27:
For any Anubis in need of a vacation, now is the ideal time to get away. This is also the perfect phase for romance.

HORUS September 28 – October 27:
In the phase of Horus, Anubis people may profit by ignoring their usual reticence concerning risk ventures. It is a period of luck in matters of chance.

WADJET October 28 – November 26:
Wadjet is a phase of sudden or unexpected news for Anubis. During this period, Anubis may be taken completely by surprise. For any Anubis seeking new friendships or partnerships this can be an especially favourable time.

SEKHMET November 27 – December 26:
For Anubis, the fire-breathing Sekhmet brings imaginative insight. Anubis people are likely to be inspired by new and fruitful ideas. This is a positive time for any change of job or location.

THE SPHINX December 27 – January 25:
This can be an emotionally trying phase for Anubis. It is not the best time to make important practical or romantic decisions.

SHU January 26 – February 24:
The Shu phase is often the most uneventful in Anubis's year. The god of the air is normally way out of reach for Anubis – so also are progress and opportunity.

ISIS February 25 – March 26:
Many Anubis people find that the Isis phase brings luck and welcome news. It is a time of good fortune.

OSIRIS March 27 – April 25:
Anubis is often frustrated by acquaintances who are not as far-sighted as they are. During the elusive Osiris phase, this can be particularly true. Anubis people may find it especially hard to convince others of their ideas or point of view.

AMUN April 26 – May 25:
Amun and Anubis are both signs favourable for business and enterprise. In financial matters, Anubis is often at their best during an Amun phase. It is a time when hard work and dedication may finally pay off.

HATHOR May 26 – June 24:
New friendships or relationships are possible and old acquaintances may be renewed. Few Anubis people have problems during a Hathor phase. Even if difficulties should arise, Anubis people are well placed to handle problems that befall them.

THE PHOENIX June 25 – July 24:
The influence of the fiery Phoenix may result in headstrong actions for Anubis. They should take care about saying more than they should, to avoid giving offence without intent.

ANUBIS July 25 – August 28:
Anubis works well during their own phase, although friendships and relationships may suffer. Anubis people could find themselves having to work so hard that they exclude their loved ones from their busy schedule.

Part Two
The Magical Workings

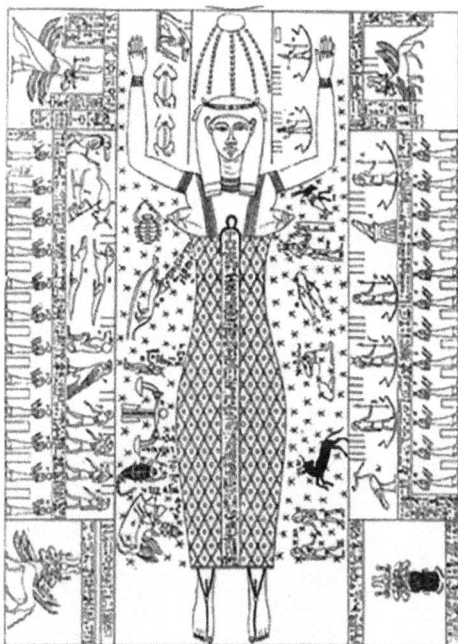

Priestess Making an Offering
Relief at Temple of Dendera

Egyptian Magic

Perhaps the most appropriate title for this section is Egyptian-*flavoured* magic, because so little remains of how the Ancient Egyptians actually worked with their deities in a magical sense. Much more has been preserved concerning official ceremonies for pharaohs, queens and high-ranking officials, as well as images of the afterlife and the detailed arrangements people had for entering it, but little can be found describing how ordinary people interacted with the gods. Talismans, and a few scraps of parchment and stelae, survive, which tell us that the lives of Ancient Egyptians were permeated with magical – some might say superstitious – beliefs. They constantly sought to appease and seek favour from their gods and goddesses.

The magical workings given in this book can be seen as a primer for interacting with the deities associated with the Egyptian natal signs. The rituals are simple and to the point – focusing upon the aspects represented by each deity in the phase over which they preside.

Neteru and Animal Likenesses

Unlike the gods and goddesses of other belief systems around the world, the deities of Ancient Egypt rarely had set stories or myths associated with them. The more consistent myths generally derive from later periods of Egypt's history, when its culture had been penetrated by the influence of other cultures, such as Greek and Roman, usually through conquest.

There is also a bewildering amount of deities, as it appears each local community had their own, or variants of the better-known gods. All the lioness-headed goddesses, for example, could be viewed as derivatives of Sekhmet, local interpretations of this fierce goddess.

The truth is that the Egyptians believed that all their gods and goddesses were Neteru, manifestations of Neter, which in essence was the Divine in all things. Neteru can be imagined as its agents on earth, or vessels shaped by human imagination that Neter could inhabit.

A wide misconception is that the Ancient Egyptians worshipped statues of their gods, even dressing them and leaving food and drink out for them to consume. But it's important to realise that these were symbolic acts. What the priests attempted to do was *persuade* Neter to enter into a vessel of stone – a statue carved in a suitable likeness – so that they could communicate more easily with it. Neter had endless variations; it comprised the many faces that some cultures called god and others called the source of all life: the living energy of the universe.

Gods and goddesses who were depicted as having the heads of animals weren't thought of as literally being cat, jackal or lioness deities, or whatever other animal they portrayed. It was simply believed that the characteristics of certain animals were pertinent to particular Neteru. A lioness might be the sacred animal of Sekhmet, because it represented her characteristics, and she might be portrayed as having the head of a lioness to demonstrate this connection, but this doesn't mean she was worshipped specifically as a goddess of lionesses. She was as fierce as a lioness, and potentially as dangerous. One look at her regal leonine head leaves us in no doubt about this trait.

When working with these ancient deities, it's best to regard the animal and symbol associations as a kind of catalogue. They help you determine what kind of characteristics you'll be working with and to choose the most appropriate Neter for the task in hand.

Magical Workings with the Deities of the Phases of the Year

For each working, you'll find information concerning the correspondences for each Neter – which stones, flowers and herbs are relevant to each sign. These correspondences are not drawn from Western astrology, but from the ancient system of the Tree of Life, or Cabbala. The Cabbala is believed to have been used by the ancient Israelites but, more importantly in this case, archaeological discoveries made at Amarna in Central Egypt have suggested that this ancient magical system might even have originated with the mysterious Egyptian pharaoh, Akhenaten. As the Cabbala provides a clear and comprehensive 'map' of the universe and the human psyche, it seemed appropriate to use this system as a basis for the sign correspondences.

A working has been devised for the deity of each phase of the year. This includes a prayer or invocation that calls upon the 'flavour' of the relevant Neter, the god or goddess who presides over it.

You can commune with the deity of your particular sign at any time. For example, if you are a 'Thoth', born between August 29 and September 27, you could perform a small working whenever you feel in need of calling upon Thoth's divine help, for protection or inspiration. Thoth's energy is of particular importance to creative people, journalists or writers. Even if you weren't born in the phase of Thoth, you can still ask him for help, at any time. However, the most potent time to approach him is at the time of year when his influence is strongest, i.e. the phase over which he rules. But you can perform any of the workings, at any time, regardless of which sign you were born under. The Neteru all possess particular 'specialities', which sometimes might be of significance to you, and what might be happening in your life, but all Neteru share the qualities of protection and helpfulness, and can be called upon whenever you need their strength.

Before performing a working, learn the correspondences for the sign. If we use Thoth as an example again, make sure you have as many of the appropriate items (such as a stone, flower, herb) and construct a small altar by arranging these items around a central orange candle (Thoth's colour). You can use a small table for this, or a shelf. The Ancient Egyptians made offerings to their deities of food they believed the gods particularly liked. In keeping with this idea, place a relevant offering of food, (in this case, a segmented orange), arranged in a small dish or bowl on your altar. The gods were also supposed to be extremely fond of perfume, so you should burn a scented oil, incense or joss stick of the pertinent flavour. Bark, leaves, fruit or flowers of Thoth's personal tree can also be included in your altar arrangement. If you're unable to gather all these items, just use as many as you can. Choose a scent or colour closest to those given in the correspondences.

Correspondences were very important to the Ancient Egyptians. They believed that things of like colour or flavour shared the same magical properties, so you can use any orange items if that's all you can get.

You can add as many personal touches to the altar as you like, including a small statue of Thoth (if you have one) or else a picture of him. (The hieroglyphic symbols for the Neteru that appear in each list of correspondences can be used as templates, which you can copy.) You can use an altar cloth of the pertinent colour, or place other items upon it that you feel are appropriate – for example, ornaments, feathers or stones of Thoth's colour.

When you are ready, sit comfortably before your altar. Have soft music playing in the background that seems right for the occasion. Breathe deeply and slowly for a minute or so, with your eyes closed. This helps alter your state of consciousness, so you're in the right, meditative frame of mind. Then, follow the instructions for the short meditation known as a pathworking. During this, you'll visualise meeting with Thoth and asking for his help

Appropriate locations to be visualised, and basic descriptions of them, are given in the instructions for each working, and where it seems most useful, illustrations are provided of certain sites. But you can research to acquire more detail, should you find this helpful.

When you have finished your working, you should eat a segment of the orange. It is said that the gods can experience earthly pleasures through humans, so it's like giving Thoth a taste of the fruit. Make an offering of what is left by throwing it over your garden, or some other patch of earth, for wild animals to consume.

The invocations for each sign have the same basic framework. They are not word for word facsimiles of invocations used by Egyptian priests, but some include known titles for the Neteru and others contain relevant Egyptian words and phrases. Often, the use of an Ancient Egyptian-English dictionary provided the inspiration needed, coupled a little creativity and imagination. This is something you can do yourself too. The thought behind the invocations are what's important, not the ancient meaning of the sounds. In essence, when creating an invocation in this way, *you* decide the meaning in advance. You can expand upon or adapt the invocations given in the book to include particular situations for which you would like help or inspiration. The most important aspect of doing magical work of this kind is the amount of will and intention you put into it.

As to the suggestions for why you might perform the workings to each god or goddess, these are merely that – suggestions. There will inevitably be dilemmas, obstructions and problems in people's lives that aren't covered here, but you should use your own intuition and feelings to decide which of the Neteru of the phases most suits your situation, and if necessary adapt the ritual to be appropriate to your particular circumstances.

Magical Morality

When working magic of any kind, it's essential to be honest with yourself. If you feel slighted or hurt, how much of the situation that led to this feeling was of your own doing? Magic should not be used for revenge or to gain unfair power or advantage over another. You should not attempt to bend another's will to your favour through ritual – rather you should aim for circumstances and coincidence to align naturally to better your situation. Negative magic to avenge hurts generally backfires because it stems from a position of weakness – feeling wounded and bitter, and sometimes being dishonest and petty. And if you are consumed by such feelings, you're not in a good position to focus on positive outcomes for yourself. Plus, how can you be a whole and happy person if all you're capable of is wishing ill on others?

If your heart is broken, ask for help mend it – forget who did the breaking. If rivals seem to have better luck than you do, and you feel resentful, work on improving your own luck and opportunities. If someone has done bad things to you, ask for protection, so they may no longer touch your life in any way. Ask for healing so that the hurt will fade and the past will no longer affect you in that way.

You should work magic to rise above the trivialities of the world, not to wallow in their murkiest depths, because that will impede or halt self-evolution. Magic should always move towards expansion, compassion, awareness and self-knowledge.

The Astronomical Ceiling
From the Temple of Hathor, Dendera

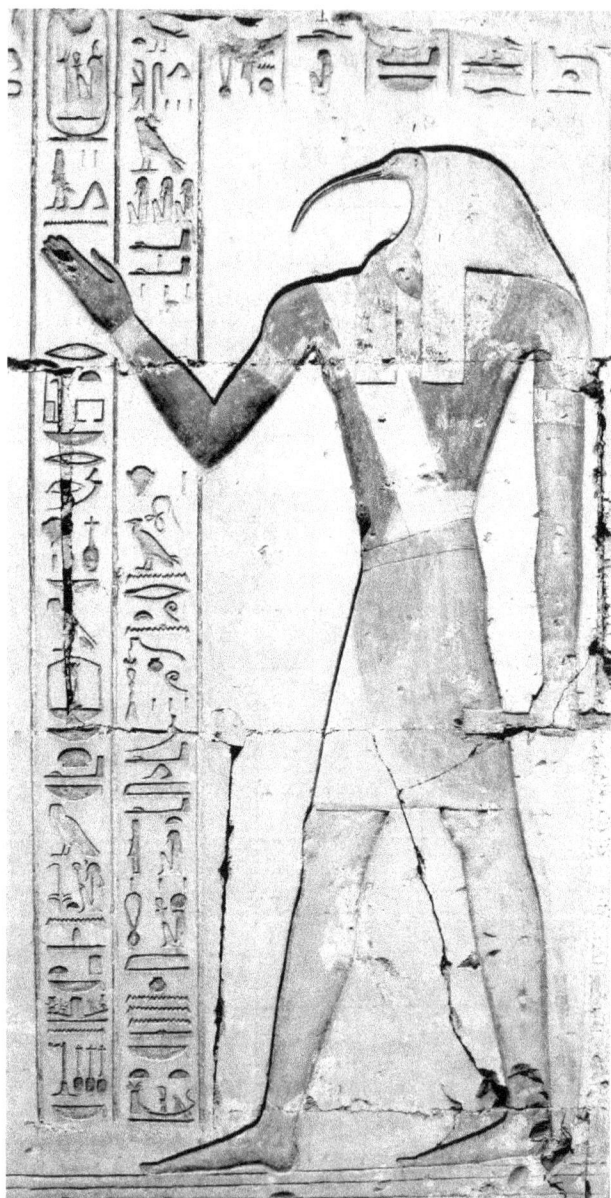

Thoth
Relief from the Temple of Rameses II, Abydos

Communing with Thoth

Thoth influence assists with matters of law, creativity, the initiation of projects, and the signing of contracts and other legal documents. Creative people may ask for inspiration and the determination to see projects through to completion. Thoth is a perfect deity to approach in matters of artistic block. His phase is also a good time to ask for help concerning disputes. Thoth restores and maintains equilibrium. One of his characteristics as an Egyptian god was to mediate between good and evil, ensuring neither got the upper hand, thus ensuring balance. He was responsible for both physical and moral law and the correct use of Ma'at, (personified by his wife of the same name), which was the force that maintained the universe.

Thoth Attributes:
Arbitration, writing, imagination, scientific breakthroughs, the arts of magic, inspiration, removal of creative blockages, restoring and maintaining equilibrium, resolution of legal matters.

Thoth Correspondences:

Stone	carnelian
Tree	quince
Food	orange
Herb	thyme
Flower	marigold
Colour	orange
Number	8
Incense	lavender
Animal	ibis
Symbol	

Other symbols: moon disk, papyrus scroll, reed pens, writing palette, stylus, ibis, baboon, scales

Thoth Working

Light the candle and incense/oil and compose yourself before your altar.

Close your eyes and breathe deeply for a couple of minutes, calming yourself, and casting off everyday thoughts and cares.

Visualisation

Imagine that you are seated in a cool temple building, protected from the fierce heat of the sun outside. You can smell incense and hear the sound of people around you working with stylus and papyrus – you are in a room of scribes.

Stand up and walk from this room – your companions don't pause from their work to see you leave. You walk along a dark corridor and eventually emerge into a smaller room where there is a statue of Thoth that dominates the enclosed space. At the feet of this statue, scented oil burns in shallow bowls, and you can see that offerings have been left there also. A soft light glimmers from lamps set upon the floor.

Raise your arms and recite the invocation to Thoth:

"Oh Thoth, Tehuti,
Who is thrice great,
I call upon you.
Protect me from all ills that approach from the east.
O Thoth, Master of Divine Words,
Protect me from all ills that approach from the south.
Tehuti, Lord of Truth,
Protect me from all ills that approach from the west.
Great Thoth, Scribe of the Gods,
Protect me from all ills that approach from the north.
Oh Thoth, Who is Mighty in Speech,
Remain at all times about me,
O Tehuti sesh-sa, sesh sa, sesh sa.

Lord of the Sacred Words,
When I cannot hear, lead me.
Lord of Khemennu, Self-Created,
When I cannot see, show me the way.
Guardian of the Sacred Books in the House of the Life,
Let me recognise and seize the opportunities that I am granted.
Let your hand work through me.
Guide me to my path of destiny.
Grant me now your power.
Tehuti, sesh-sa, sesh sa, sesh sa."

(Egyptian Pronunciation: sesh-sah
Meaning: sesh: scribe, wisdom; Saa: to know, also an alternative name
for Thoth)

Imagine that your words have called the Neter into his statue, so you might commune with him more intimately. In your mind, show Thoth precise pictures of the matter that concerns you, and how you wish it to be resolved. If you need inspiration for creative work, visualise yourself involved in this work, free of any constraint or blockage. See yourself fully enjoying the work and being productive.

Should your request be to do with legal matters, or of arbitration, visualise the situation and its participants carefully, and ask for Thoth's wise judgement. (Note that if you should have selfish or unjust reasons for this request, Thoth will not help you. It's vital to be honest with yourself over this.)

Make sure you visualise exactly how you want your future to be, so that Thoth can see these images in your mind clearly.

Whatever you're asking for, show everyone connected with the situation content and unharmed by whatever occurs.

When you are finished, thank Thoth for his aid. Breathe slowly and deeply and imagine that your visualised surroundings fade away, to be replaced by your environment in the real world. When you are ready, open your eyes.

The Earth God Geb with his Grandson Horus
Relief from Tomb KV14, Valley of the Kings

Communing with Horus

Horus promotes inventiveness and creative solutions to situations or problems. He is as swift as a hawk and this trait can be called upon and reflected in your thoughts.

This phase is also most propitious for matters involving any kind of risk or gamble. At this time, the dice might be more inclined to roll in your favour.

The creativity associated with Horus isn't so much to do with artistic endeavours precisely, (although his influence can be called upon for them), but rather to do with creative thinking in general. Perhaps there are dilemmas in your life, or new projects at work, that require some inspired ideas.

Horus is also a Neter associated with compassion and wisdom, and there will be times in life when those influences might sorely be needed. If the good of others is at stake – whether through one person's actions or decisions, or the pronouncements of a committee of some kind – Horus's innate altruism can be invoked to sway the outcome in a favourable direction for all.

When performing a ritual to Horus, it's appropriate to make wide and sweeping gestures with the arms, mimicking the movements of a falcon's wings. Imagine that these gestures help create the positive outcome you wish to achieve.

Horus Attributes:
Inventiveness, courage, altruism, creativity, compassionate wisdom, unconventional thinking, risk-taking.

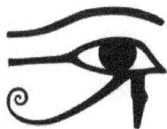

Horus Correspondences:

Stone	citrine
Tree	acacia
Food	sunflower seeds
Herb	rosemary
Flower	carnation
Colour	yellow gold
Lucky number	6
Incense	frankincense
Animal	falcon
Symbol	

Horus Working

Light the candle and incense/oil and compose yourself before your altar.

Close your eyes and breathe deeply for a couple of minutes, calming yourself, and casting off everyday thoughts and cares.

Visualisation

Imagine that you are standing outside a city built upon the edge of the western bank of the Nile – the city is Nekhen, dedicated to the falcon god Horus. The time of day is evening. You see the sun going down, a huge red globe dropping beneath the western horizon behind the city. You look up and see that in the sky a falcon is gliding on the air.

Raise your arms and recite the invocation to Horus:

"Oh Horus, great Heru,
Who is Lord of the Sky,
I call upon you.
Protect me from all ills that approach from the east.
O Horus, Dweller in the Shrine,
Protect me from all ills that approach from the south.

Heru, Pillar of Isis,
Protect me from all ills that approach from the west.
Great God of Two-Fold strength,
Protect me from all ills that approach from the north.
O Horus, Beauteous Face of Heaven,
Remain at all times about me

O Heru, Pa-neb-tawy,
Lord of the Two Lands,
When I cannot hear, lead me.
Charioteer of the Celestial Sphere,
When I cannot see, show me the way.
Heru, Bringer of Light, Banisher of Darkness,
Let me recognise and seize the opportunities that I am granted.
O Horus, Helmsman of the Divine Barge,
Let your hand work through me.
Guide me to my path of destiny.
Grant me now your power.
O Heru, Pa-neb-tawy."

(Egyptian Pronunciation: pah-*neb*-tar-*wee*
Meaning: Lord of the Two Lands 'neb' lord; 'tawy' two lands.)

The falcon hovers over you, as if it has heard your words. You see then, in the sky, that the outline of a falcon-headed man appears around the bird. This sinks down towards you, until it solidifies right in front of you – Horus has come to listen to your desires.

In your mind, show Horus precise images of the matter that concerns you, and how you want it to be resolved. If you wish for creative inspiration, in whatever regard, show the results of this inspiration and how it will positively affect your life.

Should you be asking for luck in matters of chance, show this literally in an image of dice being rolled and the numbers you asked for being revealed. Imagine the dice rolling for the situation you're thinking of.

If you are seeking Horus's help concerning a need for compassion and altruism, show him all participants in the problem and then see those people changing their mind to a fairer viewpoint. It's essential you don't visualise these people being punished or crushed, but merely finding another way that benefits everybody, including themselves.

Make sure you visualise exactly how you want your future to be, so that Horus can see these images in your mind clearly.

Whatever you're asking for, show everyone connected with the situation content and unharmed by whatever occurs.

When you are finished, thank Horus for his aid and see him depart. Breathe slowly and deeply and imagine that your visualised surroundings fade away, to be replaced by your environment in the real world. When you are ready, open your eyes.

Horus in the Form of a Falcon
Statue from the Temple at Edfu

Wadjet in the Form of a Woman, Crowning a Pharaoh
Relief from the Temple of Kom Ombo

Communing with Wadjet

Wadjet is a goddess of patience and wisdom. Her phase is propitious for all matters concerning a need to 'play a long game', as well as knowing when is the right moment to act. When the serpent strikes, she does so swiftly.

Wadjet encourages logical thought and scientific investigation, rather than relying on emotion and intuition. This influence is beneficial in matters where emotion has taken the upper hand and problems have been caused by impatience and a lack of thinking though. You can call upon Wadjet to ease such situations, to bring them back to a more logical process and to calm hysterical reactions and fears. She can also be asked to help facilitate research, and her wisdom can be brought to bear upon volatile situations.

In magical workings to Wadjet, it's appropriate to use sinuous gestures of the arms to emulate the lithe movements of a serpent.

Wadjet Attributes:
Patience, wisdom, problem-solving, realism, logic, material rather than spiritual views, objectivity, investigation, research.

Wadjet Correspondences:

Stone	amethyst
Tree	ash
Food	lemon
Herb	mustard
Flower	hyacinth
Colour	lilac
Lucky number	10
Incense	rose
Animal	serpent
Symbol	

Wadjet Working

Light the candle and incense/oil and compose yourself before your altar.

Close your eyes and breathe deeply for a couple of minutes, calming yourself, and casting off everyday thoughts and cares.

Visualisation

Imagine that you are walking through the reeds at the edge of the Nile Delta, where the great river separates into a network of tributaries and flows into the Mediterranean Sea. Nearby is the city of Per-Wadjet, sacred to the goddess Wadjet. The time is early evening; the sun is beginning to sink and shadows are long. You seek the goddess in the papyrus plants, as one of her names is 'the Papyrus-Coloured One', which refers to the green of that plant. As you walk, you are aware of being watched, and perhaps catch the faintest hiss of a snake. Now you come to a spot you feel is appropriate and recite the prayer to Wadjet.

"Oh Wadjet,
Great Lady of Heaven, I call upon you.
Protect me from all ills that approach from the east.
O Uatchet, Solar and Eternal Serpent,
Protect me from all ills that approach from the south.
O Wadjet, Dweller in the Stone of Kadesh,
Protect me from all ills that approach from the west.
Great Goddess, Mother of Nefertum the Beautiful,
Protect me from all ills that approach from the north.
O Wadjet, Opener of the Way,
Remain at all times about me.
Wadjet, Uatch-ah-ti, Uatch-ah-ti.

O Wadjet, Mistress of all the Gods,
When I cannot hear, lead me.
When I cannot see, show me the way.
O Uatchet, who came forth from Horus,

To adorn the head of Ra,
Let me recognise and seize the opportunities that I am granted.
O Wadjet, Power of the Uraeus,
Let your hand work through me.
Guide me to my path of destiny.
Grant me now your power.
Wadjet, Uatch-ah-ti, Uatch-ah-ti."

(Egyptian Pronunciation: Wadj-*aah-tee*
Meaning: Green of eyes or strong-sighted.)

A slim green snake emerges from the reeds and, as you gaze upon it, it gradually increases in size and rears up before you on its tail. It now has the head of a beautiful woman, which hangs swaying before you. The goddess regards you with wise eyes. If you are caught in a conflict and need her assistance, show her in images the whole situation. Visualise that her wise and calming influence flows over everyone and everything involved and that tensions begin to relax. Visualise the desired outcome, with everyone content.

If you seek her aid in solving a problem, or working out a puzzle in your work, feel her logical intelligence entering your mind, allowing you to walk upon different pathways within it, discover new solutions that you've not thought of before. Or perhaps Wadjet can bring someone into your life you can help you. Show her all these possibilities, with a positive outcome.

Because she is cool and serene, Wadjet can also help you conquer fears and anxieties. You can call for her presence within you if you have to face any kind of stressful situation.

Make sure you visualise exactly how you want your future to be, so that Wadjet can see these images in your mind clearly. Whatever you're asking for, show everyone connected with the situation content and unharmed by whatever occurs.

When finished, thank Wadjet for her aid and see her depart. Breathe slowly and deeply and imagine that your visualised surroundings fade away, to be replaced by your environment in the real world. When you are ready, open your eyes.

Sekhmet Statue
at the Temple of Ptah, Karnak

Communing with Sekhmet

Sekhmet is a fierce and fearless goddess, who can be called upon to make you stronger in situations where you might feel powerless. In ancient times, she was summoned to smite enemies, and while modern practitioners of magic would no longer consider that appropriate, Sekhmet's influence can be invoked as a protection. Few would dare to try and get past the snarling lioness as she stands guard beside you. If you feel threatened, Sekhmet can be called upon at any time to protect you.

Sekhmet also grants intelligent and creative thought, and the clear-sightedness to appreciate your positive qualities and use them with confidence. She is, in fact, the appropriate goddess to call upon to find that self-esteem.

In her healing aspect, Sekhmet is the 'big guns' of restorative influences. She can be approached to help those who are very ill and to smite disease. In this case, her smiting properties are entirely appropriate – not in bringing death or injury but in purging a person of disease.

Sekhmet Attributes:
Protection, strength, intelligence, clear-sightedness, objectivity, self-confidence, healing.

Sekhmet Correspondences:

Stone	Tiger's Eye
Tree	sandalwood
Food	cinnamon
Herb	pepper
Flower	poppy
Colour	red
Number	5
Incense	Red sandalwood
Animal	lioness
Symbol	

Sekhmet Working

Light the candle and incense/oil and compose yourself before your altar.

Close your eyes and breathe deeply for a couple of minutes, calming yourself, and casting off everyday thoughts and cares.

Visualisation

Imagine that you are out in the Egyptian desert, during the day, walking along the bottom of a wadi, which is a valley or dry riverbed that only contains water at certain times of year. Now is the dry season. Sekhmet is known as 'Goddess at the Mouth of the Wadi' so you seek her in this place. When you look up you can see that lionesses are lying lazily on the high banks to either side, watching you, but you don't feel threatened by them. They guard you as you approach the goddess.

Eventually you come to an oasis and here you raise your arms and recite the invocation to Sekhmet:

"O Sekhmet,
Lady of the Bright Red Linen,
I call upon you.
Protect me from all ills that approach from the east.
O Lion Star, Lady of the Place of the Beginning of Time,
Protect me from all ills that approach from the south.
O Sekhmet, Lady of the Many Faces,
Protect me from all ills that approach from the west.
O Gold, Lady of the Waters of Life,
Protect me from all ills that approach from the north.
O Sekhmet, Ruler of the Chamber of Flames,
Remain at all times about me
Sekhet-Aahkut-Nebat, Sekhet-Aahkut-Nebat.

O Sekhmet, Most Beautiful Among the Neteru,
When I cannot hear, lead me.
When I cannot see, show me the way.

O Sekhmet, Shining of Countenance,
Let me recognise and seize the opportunities that I am granted.
O Sekhmet, Adorable One,
Let your hand work through me.
Guide me to my path of destiny.
Grant me now your power.
Sekhet-Aahkut-Nebat, Sekhet-Aahkut-Nebat.

(Egyptian Pronunciation: Sek-*ett* Aah-*cut* Neb-*at*
Meaning: Sekhmet of the Flaming Eye)

After you have finished speaking, you realise that Sekhmet now sits in the shade of the palm trees by the oasis, with lionesses lying around her. She is dressed in bright red linen and has the head of a lioness. You are aware of her great power but approach her fearlessly.

If you are here to ask for Sekhmet's strength, show her clear images of how this will manifest in your life, how you want things to be. Imagine yourself in situations you generally find intimidating and stressful and see yourself standing tall and strong and coping with them. See yourself able to deal with people who might seek to put you down. You have Sekhmet's clear sight to disarm them with words, without being emotional.

If you seek protection, show Sekhmet images of your situation and everyone involved in it. If you feel threatened, show antagonists as vicious dogs who are now losing interest in their prey, moving away cravenly, tails between their legs. They fear a greater power even if they're not sure what it is. Best to leave it alone! Their power to harm is taken from them.

If you're appealing to Sekhmet's healing aspect, show her images of who is ill or hurt – yourself if that's pertinent – and then see Sekhmet lay her hands upon this person, casting out disease and sickness. See this person purged as if by cleansing fire and being whole, healthy and happy.

Make sure you visualise exactly how you want your future

to be, so that Sekhmet can see these images in your mind clearly. Whatever you're asking for, show everyone connected with the situation content and unharmed by whatever occurs.

When you are finished, thank Sekhmet for her aid and see her depart.

Breathe slowly and deeply and imagine that your visualised surroundings fade away, to be replaced by your environment in the real world. When you are ready, open your eyes.

Sekhmet
From a Relief at the Temple Complex at Kom Ombo

Egyptian Sphinx
The Louvre, Paris

Communing with the Sphinx

The Sphinx, also known in Ancient Egypt as Hu, is a creature of mystery, whatever cultural tradition they're found in. They are also extremely clever. There are several kinds of sphinxes – creatures with the body of a lion and the head of a different creature, and sometimes the wings of a bird. In Egyptian mythology, criosphinxes had the head of a ram and hieracosphinxes the head of a hawk. Hu is an androsphinx, meaning he has the head of a man. His phase is propitious for matters requiring inventive thought and problem-solving, and also for gaining insight into situations that might otherwise be elusive.

Hu is also associated with all types of initiatory experiences, whether that should pertain to magic or simply experiences in life that in themselves involve a kind of initiation, a transformation of being. This might include dramatic changes within your life, where you take up a new career or lifestyle. Sometimes, you reach a crossroads in life, where you could do with insight as to how the different roads might affect you and what outcomes you can expect from your decisions. Hu can illuminate these paths.

There might also be situations where you could do with some of the Sphinx's mystery and allure yourself – to intrigue others, perhaps, when you have ideas or projects you want them to support, so they think "this person is interesting. What they have to offer will surely be interesting too."

Hu also has a guardian aspect – more of a solid, impassable presence than that of fire-breathing Sekhmet. He can be called upon to confound antagonists, to make them feel there are too many obstacles to pass to get to you.

Sphinx Attributes:
Mystery, inventiveness, guardianship, initiatory experiences, cleverness, intuitiveness, problem-solving, gaining insight, creation of opportunities.

Sphinx Correspondences:

Stone	quartz
Tree	almond
Food	white grapes
Herb	coriander
Flower	lily
Colour	white
Number	1
Incense	eucalyptus
Psychic power	clairvoyance
Animal	lion
Symbol	

Sphinx Working

Light the candle and incense/oil and compose yourself before your altar.

Close your eyes and breathe deeply for a couple of minutes, calming yourself, and casting off everyday thoughts and cares.

Visualisation

Imagine that you are on the plateau of Giza at night-time. Here, the great pyramids stand, and also the statue of the sphinx. Your environment is not how Giza is now, but how it used to be thousands of years ago – when the Sphinx was new and undamaged, and there were no tourists or modern buildings and vehicles to spoil the landscape.

You find yourself alone upon the plateau. The air is pleasantly warm and fragrant. Above you, the sky is encrusted with stars, unsullied by light pollution. You feel as if the world is young and fresh, and full of magical power.

As you stand before the great statue, raise your arms and recite the invocation to Hu:

"O Hu,
Watcher of the Dawn,
I call upon you.
Protect me from all ills that approach from the east.
Lord of Heliopolis,
Protect me from all ills that approach from the south.
O Hu, Gatekeeper of the Silences,
Protect me from all ills that approach from the west.
Great Lion, Guardian of the Rising Sun,
Protect me from all ills that approach from the north.
O Hu, Lord of the Resting Places,
Remain at all times about me.
Tep-Neb-Rostau, Tep-Neb-Rostau, Tep-Neb-Rostau.

O Hu, Light on the Mighty River,
When I cannot hear, lead me.
O Hu, Sentinel of the Gateway of the Duat,
When I cannot see, show me the way.
O Hu, Guardian of the Road to Rostau,
Let me recognise and seize the opportunities that I am granted.
O Hu, Mighty One,
Let your hand work through me.
Guide me to my path of destiny.
Grant me now your power.
Tep-Neb-Rostau, Tep-Neb-Rostau, Tep-Neb-Rostau."

(Egyptian Pronunciation: Tep-Neb-Ross-tow (as in owl)
Meaning: Guardian of the Road to Rostau, the road to the underworld.)

When you've finished your invocation, you see that a shape is approaching you through the darkness, from the shadow of the great statue. This is Hu in living form, an immense lion, who has the head of a handsome man and wears the head-dress of a pharaoh. When he stands before you, his head is level with your own.

197

Show the Sphinx images of what you require from him. You might wish him to create enigmas or solve them. You might wish for knowledge where there is only shadow.

If you seek him to initiate change, show him how you want to be at the conclusion of this change – content, fulfilled and happy. Given Hu's nature, it's not necessary to visualise the processes of this change, only the outcome. Hu himself will direct the process.

If you wish for the Sphinx's air of mystery, visualise this as a cloak he gives to you, and which you wrap around yourself. Imagine it as imbued with his attributes, which now shine from you too.

Make sure you visualise exactly how you want the end result to be, so that Hu can see these images in your mind clearly. If appropriate, show everyone connected with the situation being content and unharmed by whatever occurs.

When you are finished, thank Hu for his aid and see him depart.

Breathe slowly and deeply and imagine that your visualised surroundings fade away, to be replaced by your environment in the real world. When you are ready, open your eyes.

The Sphinx
Giza

Shu Welcoming the Pharaoh, Rameses III
Relief from The House of Eternity, Thebes

Communing with Shu

Shu was the god of the air and its winds, and has aspects of movement, as well as promoting tranquillity and health, particularly mental health. His qualities are reviving. There are many situations upon which Shu's traits can be brought to bear. His cool, restoring winds can clear paths and blow away cobwebs, bringing clarity and forward movement. His aspect of peace-maker can initiate calm and resolve hot-headed disputes.

This Neter also represents creativity, and the swift blooming of ideas. His attributes are conducive to furthering creative projects, especially those associated with public performance. Shu's influence is extremely beneficial to such ventures, bringing an ambience of liveliness and inventiveness.

In the settling of disputes, Shu's strength is a cleansing air of serenity, so that tempers cool down and those involved are able to view the situation with objectivity rather than hot emotion.

In his healing aspect, Shu is particularly effective concerning afflictions of the mind.

Shu Attributes:
Peace-making, calming, innovative, reviving, cleansing, healing – especially of the mind.

Shu Correspondences:

Stone	moonstone
Tree	silver birch
Food	lychee
Herb	lemon balm
Flower	Iris
Colour	purple
Lucky number	9
Incense	white sandalwood
Animal	swallow
Symbol	

Shu Working

Light the candle and incense/oil and compose yourself before your altar.

Close your eyes and breathe deeply for a couple of minutes, calming yourself, and casting off everyday thoughts and cares.

Visualisation

Imagine that you are standing upon a hilltop in the dry desert of Ancient Egypt. It is morning, and the wind blows against you, making you feel a rising sense of imminence, as if something approaches you. Throwing back your head, you gaze into the sky, so vast and empty, but for the birds that wheel high upon the breezes.

Raise your arms and recite the invocation to Shu:

"O Shu,
Bearer of the Sky,
I call upon you.
Protect me from all ills that approach from the east.
Divine Twin, Lord of the Firmament,
Protect me from all ills that approach from the south.
O Shu, Wings of the Silver Clouds,
Protect me from all ills that approach from the west.
O Shu, Brother and Consort of Tefnut,
Protect me from all ills that approach from the north.
O Shu, God of Light by Day and Moon by Night,
Remain at all times about me.
Hinu-en-Shu-Nefer, Hinu-en-Shu-Nefer.

O Shu, Master of the Cool Winds and Breezes,
When I cannot hear, lead me.
O Shu, Conjuror of a Thousand Years,
When I cannot see, show me the way.

O Shu, Lord of the Sun in Summer,
Let me recognise and seize the opportunities that I am granted.
O Shu, Sweet Swallow of Salvation,
Let your hand work through me.
Guide me to my path of destiny.
Grant me now your power.
Hinu-en-Shu-Nefer, Hinu-en-Shu-Nefer."

(Egyptian Pronunciation: Hin-*oo* en *shoo* nef-*er*
Meaning: Palace of Shu the Beautiful – meaning here atmosphere or air of Shu.)

Wispy clouds form above you, and gradually you perceive within them the form of the god. He is a cloud himself, composed of air and the moisture of his sister-wife Tefnut, which makes him visible to you. Show Shu images of what you require of him. If this is to do with a creative or dramatic project, show him how you wish this work to be received well by all, so it will be successful and lead to greater opportunities.

Should you wish him to solve a dispute, show him every angle of the argument and ask for his calming influence to expel negativity and angry emotions. If people need to talk calmly together, ask for this to be made possible.

If you seek Shu's aid concerning mental illness, stress or anxiety, visualise that his cooling, healing attributes cure and restore the person concerned, (yourself if this is pertinent) freeing them from fear and discomfort. His serene breath brings respite and rest.

Make sure you visualise exactly how you want the end result to be, so that Shu can see these images in your mind clearly. If appropriate, show everyone connected with the situation being content and unharmed by whatever occurs.

When you are finished, thank Shu for his aid and see him depart. Breathe slowly and deeply and imagine that your visualised surroundings fade away, to be replaced by your environment in the real world. When you are ready, open your eyes.

Isis leading Queen Nefertari
Tomb Painting, Thebes

Communing with Isis

Isis's name meant 'Great of Magic' and she is therefore the ideal Neter to consult concerning any magical endeavour, or to gain wisdom upon a spiritual path. Yet her embracing nature means that she may be approached in respect of any kind of problem or request.

Isis promotes compassion and honesty and also a strong sense of fairness. The legend of her determination to recover the parts of her dismembered husband and restore him to wholeness illustrates her quality of unswerving dedication to a task and the stamina to carry it through to completion. She may therefore be petitioned to help with situations that might seem too difficult or draining to accomplish.

As a mother and wife, which are important aspects of her mythology, she is also intrinsic to matters associated with the domestic side of relationships and the physical aspects of womanhood and motherhood. She can be called upon to assist during childbirth, or to help with matters of health that are particular to women.

The Ancient Egyptians believed that knots had magical power, so amulets made of knotted cord or ribbon are appropriate gifts for a female friend or relative needing Isis's protection.

Despite her strong associations with femininity, her power extends to everyone, regardless of gender. She was regarded as the most beautiful of Neteru, radiating confidence and serenity. Asking to be instilled with these traits in any situation helps you to cope with them more capably.

Isis Attributes:
Honesty, compassion, protectiveness, magic, wisdom, beauty, justice, fairness, motherhood, and matters associated with female health.

Isis Correspondences:

Stone	lapis lazuli
Tree	sycamore
Food	avocado
Herb	tarragon
Flower	rose
Colour	green
Lucky number	7
Incense	lotus
Animal	cat
Symbol	

Other symbols associated with Isis: a throne, a sun disk with cow's horns, the sycamore tree. Animals: sparrow, cobra, vulture, and kite.

Isis Working

Light the candle and incense/oil and compose yourself before your altar.

Close your eyes and breathe deeply for a couple of minutes, calming yourself, and casting off everyday thoughts and cares.

Visualisation

Imagine that you are approaching the ancient temple dedicated to Isis at Philae, which lies on the banks of the Nile. You see the temple as it is now, partly ruined, but still possessing the power and tranquillity of an earlier era. The time is late afternoon, just as shadows are beginning to lengthen. Philae is not a vast temple complex, but a small, elegant building, lending it an intimate atmosphere.

Stand within the temple, raise your arms and recite the invocation to Isis:

Ruins of Isis's Temple at Philae

"O Isis, Lady Aset,
Mother of the Gods,
I call upon you.
Protect me from all ills that approach from the east.
She of the Double Crowns,
Protect me from all ills that approach from the south.
O Isis, Dweller in the House of the Evening,
Protect me from all ills that approach from the west.
Great Goddess of the Golden Dawn,
Protect me from all ills that approach from the north.
O Aset, Guardian of Dwellings,
Remain at all times about me.
Aset-Nefer Mut Neteru, Aset-Nefer Mut Neteru.

Mother of Horus of Gold,
When I cannot hear, lead me
O Isis, Lady of the Words of Power,
When I cannot see, show me the way.
O Isis, Queen of Mesen, Giver of Life,
Let me recognise and seize the opportunities that I am granted.
O Aset, Foremost among the Neteru,
Let your hand work through me.
Guide me to my path of destiny.
Grant me now your power.
Aset-Nefer Mut Neteru, Aset-Nefer Mut Neteru.

(Egyptian Pronunciation: Az-et Nef-er Mut Net-er-oo
Meaning: Isis the Beautiful, Mother of Gods.)

After you have spoken these words, sit down within the temple. Isis appears before you, dressed in pleated blue linen, wearing a sun disk upon her head surrounded by curving cow's horns. Her expression is that of compassion and kindness. You feel that you know her well, whether you have approached her before magically or not.

Isis is attentive to what you have to say. Show her images in your mind of your problem or question. If you approach her seeking assistance with your magical path, ask her to instil you with knowledge.

If you require her aid with matters concerning health, explain the problem to her and visualise her laying her hands on you (or another, if you seek help for them), to heal all hurts.

Isis can be asked for assistance in virtually any kind of situation; be sure to focus upon her aspects of compassion and dedication. Make sure you visualise exactly how you want the end result of your request to be, so that Isis can see these images in your mind clearly. If appropriate, show everyone connected with the situation being content and unharmed by whatever occurs.

When you are finished, thank Isis for her aid and see her depart.

Breathe slowly and deeply and imagine that your visualised surroundings fade away, to be replaced by your environment in the real world. When you are ready, open your eyes.

Osiris, Throned, with Crook and Flail
Wall Painting from the Tomb of Queen Nefertari, Thebes

Communing with Osiris

Osiris is the ideal Neter to approach concerning matters of regeneration. If a situation or ideas have become stagnant, or projects have ground to a halt, as if the energy has drained out of everything and everyone involved, then Osiris's influence can revive them.

This can apply to any circumstance where regrowth is vital, even including areas of the landscape that need restoration or redevelopment. Perhaps you have old works or projects you'd like to revive and need inspiration and help to do so.

Osiris is associated with growth in nature, so is also appropriate in respect of rearing and nurturing plants and animals. You may visualise him as having either green skin, which symbolises rebirth, or black skin, which symbolises the fertility of the soil in which all things grow.

This Neter is also the archetypal 'wise judge' so can be called upon for insight into matters that apply to other aspects of his being.

Osiris Attributes:
Wise judgement, resilience, regeneration, new growth, restoration, rebirth.

Osiris Correspondences:

Stone	moss agate
Tree	cedar
Food	pomegranate
Herb	basil
Flower	violet
Colour	silver/grey
Lucky number	2
Incense	myrrh
Animal	scarab
Symbol	𓊽

Other symbols associated with Osiris: flail, crook, ostrich feather, crown.

Osiris Working

Light the candle and incense/oil and compose yourself before your altar. Close your eyes and breathe deeply for a couple of minutes, calming yourself, and casting off everyday thoughts and cares.

Visualisation

Imagine that you are walking towards the Oseirion, which is the temple dedicated to Osiris in the ancient town of Abydos. The ruins of the temple are filled with water. It is night-time and all is still. Moonlight reflects from the pools, which by daylight are green but now appear black. Step down into the water and absorb the atmosphere of the site. Perhaps water was a part of the rites of Osiris, or maybe changes in the environment mean that what was once dry now occasionally floods. Whatever the reason, in this era, the Oseirion is a place of water, and you can associate it with the Fields of Reeds of the Underworld, where Osiris is king.

The Ruins of the Oseirion at Abydos

Raise your arms and recite the invocation to Osiris:

"O Osiris,
Lord of the Two Plumes,
I call upon you.
Protect me from all ills that approach from the east.
Asar, Guardian of Souls,
Protect me from all ills that approach from the south.
Great God, Whose Domain is the Duat,
Protect me from all ills that approach from the west.
Lord Osiris, Lord of the Hidden Chest,
Protect me from all ills that approach from the north.
Lord of Amenti, King of the Living,
Remain at all times about me.
Khnemu-ut-em-Ankh, Khnemu-ut-em-Ankh.

O Asar, Sower of the Seeds of Time,
When I cannot hear, lead me.
Asar, who dwells in Orion,
With a season in the sky and a season on the earth,
When I cannot see, show me the way.
Osiris, He of Two Thousand Years,
Let me recognise and seize the opportunities that I am granted.
Great God, Lord of Right and Truth,
Let your hand work through me.
Guide me to my path of destiny.
Grant me now your power.
Khnemu-ut-em-Ankh, Khnemu-ut-em-Ankh."

*(Egyptian Pronunciation: K-nem-oo ut em ank
Meaning: Osiris Lord of Life, Khnemu being an alternative name for him.)*

You see in the moonlight the tall figure of a man appear between the rough cut columns of the temple. He wears a tall conical crown and is swathed in the wrappings of a mummy.

He carries a flail and a crook. His face is beautiful, the eyes thickly outlined in black kohl. This is Osiris, Ruler of the Afterlife, and the Lord of Regrowth.

In your mind, show Osiris images of what you wish from him. If you are concerned growth in a business sense, give him all the information you have, and ask for his wise and fair judgement to expand your enterprise.

If you approach him for aid with the natural world – connected with the care and nurture of plants and/or animals – show Osiris the outcome you desire, the flourishing fertility that will grant success.

If you require regeneration within your life, in whatever sense, imagine clearly how you would like this revival to take effect and what the results must be.

For a true rebirth, a dramatic change, visualise casting off all that holds you back in life, and being given a clean, new start. But you must be precise, and affirm that these changes will harm none.

Whatever you are petitioning for, make sure you visualise exactly how you want the end result to be, so that Osiris can see these images in your mind clearly. If appropriate, show everyone connected with the situation being content and unharmed by whatever occurs.

When you are finished, thank Osiris for his aid and see him depart.

Breathe slowly and deeply and imagine that your visualised surroundings fade away, to be replaced by your environment in the real world. When you are ready, open your eyes.

Isis and Osiris
Relief from the Temple at Dendera

The Pharaoh Horemheb Before Amun-Ra
Statue in Luxor Museum

Communing with Amun

Amun, as a creator god, is a Neter of force and influence. He called the world into being through the power of his own mind. Should you require strength, patience and self-belief for any situation in life, Amun is the Neter to approach for assistance. In his role as sole creator, he is well-suited to nurture the seeds of projects and ideas, to manifest thought into reality.

This deity is also appropriate to help with matters concerning leadership, managing a team, or dealing with employees. His influence is neither chaotic nor hasty; he is the epitome of confident patience, having the tenacity to wait for results and see a project through. This sense of poised calm affects others in a positive way, easing any doubts they might have.

Amun also brings objectivity, a sense of realism, and his attributes are helpful when you are involved in delicate negotiations. He has the power to convince others – but only because his ideas are sound.

Amun Attributes:
Expansion, strength, tenacity, realism, negotiation, patience, faith in self, creation, leadership.

Amun Correspondences:

Stone	turquoise
Tree	oak
Food	damson
Herb	sage
Flower	blue bell
Colour	blue
Lucky number	4
Incense	cloves
Animal	ram
Symbol	

Other symbols associated with Amun: criosphinx, two long ostrich feathers.

Amun Working

Light the candle and incense/oil and compose yourself before your altar.

Close your eyes and breathe deeply for a couple of minutes, calming yourself, and casting off everyday thoughts and cares.

Visualisation

Imagine that you stand before the great temple to Amun that is part of the immense complex at Karnak. Visualise it as it was in its prime, with a roof and all its huge columns intact. The time is early morning, the sun still low on the horizon. The world is waking up.

Artistic Representation of Amun's Temple in Ancient Times

Walk into the great hall and absorb the stillness and quiet of this sacred place. The building is so huge you feel tiny within it. Raise your arms and recite the invocation to Amun:

"O Amun,
Father of the Gods,
I call upon you.
Protect me from all ills that approach from the east.

O Amun, Lord of the Hidden Abode,
Protect me from all ills that approach from the south.
King of the Four Horizons,
Protect me from all ills that approach from the west.
O Permanent One, King of the Setting Sun,
Protect me from all ills that approach from the north.
O Amun, Eternal Flame of Life,
Remain at all times about me.
Amun-neth-hep-tchet, Amun-neth-hep-tchet.

O Amun, Dweller on the Throne and Keeper of the Sceptre,
He who is rich in names,
When I cannot hear, lead me.
When I cannot see, show me the way.
O Amun, Hidden of Aspect, Mysterious of Form,
Let me recognise and seize the opportunities that I am granted.
Great God, Maker of the Two Lands,
Let your hand work through me.
Guide me to my path of destiny.
Grant me now your power.
Amun-neth-hep-tchet, Amun-neth-hep-tchet."

(Egyptian Pronunciation: Ah-*men neth* hep-*chet*
Meaning: Amun of the Hidden Abode.)

You feel a great power enter into his sanctum. The god, being the Hidden One, does not manifest before your eyes, but your other senses are aware of him. You smell incense smouldering nearby. You hear the rush of winds, because Amun is associated with calming storms at sea. You know that Amun is before you and you sense his immense form, even if you cannot see it.

If you are here to sow the seeds of creation for a new idea or project, show Amun clear, precise images of what you intend to achieve and create. Ask for his influence to empower this endeavour.

Should you seek Amun's aid with matters of business, or working in a team, ask for his strength, his ability to lead fairly and wisely, to enter into you so that others are confident to follow your lead. Ask for his wisdom to imbue your decisions.

If you wish to acquire some of Amun's qualities, such as patience and self-belief, visualise yourself having these attributes already and how they will improve your life.

If you should require his influence in situations requiring negotiation with others, visualise clearly the end result you wish to achieve.

Whatever you are petitioning for, make sure you visualise exactly how you want the end result to be, so that Amun can see these images in your mind clearly. If appropriate, show everyone connected with the situation being content and unharmed by whatever occurs.

When you are finished, thank Amun for his aid and feel his nebulous presence depart.

Breathe slowly and deeply and imagine that your visualised surroundings fade away, to be replaced by your environment in the real world. When you are ready, open your eyes.

Detail of the Temple of Amun
Naqa

Statue of Hathor
British Museum

Communing with Hathor

Hathor (or Het-Hert) is the nearest the Ancient Egyptians came to having a goddess of love – but not in the same way as deities such as Aphrodite or Venus were associated with romantic emotions and affairs. The theme of love was a component of Hathor's attributes, but she had others too.

However, she is the most suitable Neter to approach concerning matters of the heart and romantic attachments. While it's not appropriate to ask her to sway someone's feelings in your direction, since that would mean asking her to influence another's free will, you may ask for her help in smoothing the way in a new relationship, or to invite love into your life where it is lacking.

Of all the things you might ask a Neter to assist you with, love is among the trickiest. When you desire someone, you naturally want them to desire you in return, and in the heat of that feeling might consider it acceptable to go to any lengths to achieve that. However, it's unethical, and perhaps even dangerous, to impose your will magically upon another. There are often unwanted consequences, such as when the longed-for affair goes sour. If you have asked for magical aid to 'force' this relationship, to *make* someone fall in love with you, it might be difficult to separate from them should your own love wane. At the hot, hungry start of a love affair, it's unlikely you'll be thinking of a possible future separation, and may even believe that would never happen – but it might. So do be precise and careful what you ask for in this respect. You can ask Hathor to open the way to love if it's naturally possible, and to perhaps align coincidence and circumstance in your favour, but you should not ask her to influence the heart and mind of another.

Aside from this aspect, Hathor is also a Neter associated with hospitality, entertainment, music and dancing, and artistic pursuits. She can be approached in respect of instilling true emotion into creative projects, to bring them alive in a way that others will feel. Her influence around a party, or a rite of passage, such as a wedding or a coming of age, will help make the event a joyous success.

Hathor Attributes:
Love, romantic affairs, joy, artistic pursuits, particularly in music and dancing, hospitality and entertainment.

Hathor Correspondences:

Stone	jasper (green or brown)
Tree	elm
Food	olive
Herb	fennel
Flower	cowslip
Colour	ochre
Lucky number	10
Incense	patchouli
Animal	cow
Symbol	

Other symbols associated with Hathor: Animals – lioness, white cow, hippopotamus, cobra, falcon. Musical instruments, the sistrum (sacred rattle), drums. Also mirrors and pots of cosmetics.

Hathor Working

Light the candle and incense/oil and compose yourself before your altar.

Close your eyes and breathe deeply for a couple of minutes, calming yourself, and casting off everyday thoughts and cares.

Visualisation

Imagine that you are walking in daytime towards the great temple dedicated to Hathor at Dendera – an isolated spot deep in the Egyptian desert. You can see the immense columns at the front of the temple, which are decorated with heads of the goddess, who is shown having a cow's ears. The cow was a sacred animal to this Neter.

Hathor's Temple at Dendera

Enter into the cool darkness of the temple. You find yourself in the Hypostyle Hall, which has a very high ceiling, and is richly decorated throughout with colourful wall and ceiling paintings, and rows of intricately-carved columns. You can hear music, the playing of a harp, the rattle of sistra, and the beat of drums. You pass into a further chamber, which was known as the 'Hall of Appearances'. Here, raise your arms and recite the invocation to Hathor:

"O Hathor, Lady Het-Hert,
Joyful Goddess of Love, Music and Dance,
I call upon you.
Protect me from all ills that approach from the east.
O Hathor, Lady of the Universe,
Protect me from all ills that approach from the south.
Het-Hert, Keeper of the Scarab Crown,
Protect me from all ills that approach from the west.
O Hathor, Lady of the House of Jubilation,
Protect me from all ills that approach from the north.

Great Lady, Daughter of the Night,
Remain at all times about me.
Ta-senet-neferti, Ta-senet-neferti.

Lady of Eternal Love,
When I cannot hear, lead me.
O Hathor, Child of the Silver Voice,
When I cannot see, show me the way.
Het-Hert, Singer of Sweet Desert Songs,
Let me recognise and seize the opportunities that I am granted.
Great Goddess, Diamond of the Solar Disk,
Let your hand work through me.
Guide me to my path of destiny.
Grant me now your power.
Ta-senet-neferti, Ta-senet-neferti."

(Egyptian Pronunciation: Tah *sennet nef-*ur-*tee*
Meaning: The Beautiful One.)

The goddess appears before you, dressed in a softly-pleated robe of diaphanous white linen. She has the form of an extremely beautiful woman with exquisite makeup and head-dress – a solar disk surrounded by the horns of a cow. To either side of her are huge statues of recumbent white cows – beautiful, serene creatures – they too wearing the familiar black kohl makeup around their gentle eyes.

Hathor's expression holds merriment and affection. If you are here to seek her help with love, speak to her honestly about your situation and those involved.

If you wish to invite love into your life, ask her to grant you opportunities for romance, with people who are suitable for you, and who will not conceal unforeseen difficulties. Try to imagine your ideal partner – but refrain from making them so idealised they couldn't exist in reality. We all have faults, but some faults are easier to exist with than others. Ask for mutual physical attraction, affinity in outlook and like-mindedness in a partner.

To bring Hathor's joyous influence to an event, show her what's in store and how she can ensure its success, so that everyone enjoys themselves to the full.

In creative matters, show her how she can help enhance your work with feeling and passion.

Whatever you are petitioning for, make sure you visualise exactly how you want the end result to be, so that Hathor can see these images in your mind clearly. If appropriate, show everyone connected with the situation being content and unharmed by whatever occurs.

When you are finished, thank Hathor for her aid and see her depart.

Breathe slowly and deeply and imagine that your visualised surroundings fade away, to be replaced by your environment in the real world. When you are ready, open your eyes.

Hathor in the Form of a Cow

Benu Bird
Ancient Egyptian Papyrus

Communing with the Phoenix

The Phoenix, or Benu bird, is associated with rebirth, not in the sense of being reborn through the earth, but in that of 'rising from the ashes'. It represents resilience in being able to stand up again, after being knocked down by setbacks in life, and carrying on with optimism, rather than being defeatist and giving up.

You may approach the Benu when you've suffered obstructions and disappointments and ask for its eternal sense of hope and renewal, so that whatever held you back or presented an obstacle won't prevent you from dusting yourself off and carrying on.

The Phoenix, with its sense of adventure and vitality is also appropriate when you wish to bring these qualities into your life.

The Benu cannot be destroyed; it represents an eternal cycle. There might be many times in life when this attribute is both appropriate and beneficial.

Phoenix Attributes:
Optimism, seizing opportunities, hope, renewal and rebirth in the sense of 'rising from the ashes', vitality and adventure.

Phoenix Correspondences:

Stone	amber
Tree	aloe
Food	date
Colour	indigo
Herb	nutmeg
Flower	daffodil
Lucky number	12
Incense	saffron
Animal	heron
Symbol	

Phoenix Working

Light the candle and incense/oil, and compose yourself before your altar.

Close your eyes and breathe deeply for a couple of minutes, calming yourself, and casting off everyday thoughts and cares.

Visualisation

Imagine that you are walking in the Egyptian desert in the hours before dawn. The air is cold and the terrain difficult beneath your feet. There are high mountains around you, and the sound of your footsteps echo back to you from them.

You come to a spot where a faint glow on the horizon tells you that soon the sun will rise. In this place, raise your arms and recite the invocation to the Benu Bird.

"O Benu,
The Sacred Bird Who Rises from the Flames,
I call upon you.
Protect me from all ills that approach from the east.
O Benu, Keeper of the Eternal Fire,
Protect me from all ills that approach from the south.
Phoenix, Guardian of the Sacred Persea Tree,
Protect me from all ills that approach from the west.
Sun Bird of the Rising Disk,
Protect me from all ills that approach from the north.
O Benu, Sacred to the Sun God Ra,
Remain at all times about me.
Nefer-Benu-Aakhu, Nefer-Benu-Aakhu.

Beautiful Bird of Burning Flames,
When I cannot hear, lead me.
O Benu, Who Rises in Brilliance,
When I cannot see, show me the way,
Benu, Who Comes Forth From the Ashes,
Let me recognise and seize the opportunities that I am granted.

O Benu, Lord of Heliopolis, City of the Sun,
Let your eternal fire work through me.
Guide me to my path of destiny.
Grant me now your power.
Nefer-Benu-Aakhu, Nefer-Benu-Aakhu."

(Egyptian Pronunciation: Nefer Ben-*oo aah*-koo
Meaning: Beautiful bird of fire/radiance.)

The sun rises above the horizon in a glorious blaze and its light flows over the forbidding landscape. As you gaze into the sky above it, the Benu bird takes shape from the growing radiance, a magnificent and enormous bird wreathed in flame. His wise eyes gaze down upon you.

In your mind, show images to the Benu of why you seek his aid. If you have suffered a setback, you should visualise all that's occurred burning away, leaving only ashes. Then imagine that all you want to happen rises from these ashes and comes into reality before you.

If you are here to invite adventure and vitality into your life, visualise images of how you wish this to manifest.

If you wish new opportunities to arise from a stale situation, imagine the old being burned away to make way for the new.

Whatever you are petitioning for, make sure you visualise exactly how you want the end result to be, so that the Phoenix can see these images in your mind clearly. If appropriate, show everyone connected with the situation being content and unharmed by whatever occurs.

When you are finished, thank the Benu for his aid and see him fly away.

Breathe slowly and deeply and imagine that your visualised surroundings fade away, to be replaced by your environment in the real world. When you are ready, open your eyes.

Statue of Anubis
Ny Carlsberg Glyptoteket Museum, Copenhagen

Communing with Anubis

Anubis, being a guardian of graveyards and possessing a strong protective trait, is an ideal Neter to approach in respect of protection and guardianship. He was known by other names that had strong associations with his role in funerary rites, including Tepy-Dju-Ef, which meant "He Who is Upon His Mountain", denoting that he kept guard over tombs from the hills that overlooked them, and Neb-Ta-Djeser, which meant "Lord of the Sacred Land" and described his role as presiding over the desert necropolis.

For those born in his sign, he is particularly associated with deep insight and resolution, but anyone may approach him should they require these aspects to help them.

Anubis has a steadfast quality, and the ability to see through any kind of fabrication to the truth. He could be said to reveal truth through the weighing of the human heart, which was part of his function in the underworld.

Should you feel in need of strong protection, Anubis can be invoked as a guardian in the household – to watch over it while you are absent, and particularly if you feel threatened by potential break-ins or are enduring unwanted attention from someone that makes you feel threatened. Anubis stands guard, and his mere presence is usually enough to deter wrongdoers. Even if they aren't aware of what unnerves them, they might feel it and are less likely to try and enter the house. However, should you have cats living with you, it often upsets them greatly to invite the influence of Anubis into the home. In that case, Sekhmet would be more appropriate as a domestic guardian – although you should be aware her nature is to breathe fire and attack rather than stand guard and deter.

If you have to go somewhere alone and feel unsafe, you can call upon Anubis to walk with you.

Anubis Attributes:
Protection, guardianship, insight, judgement, being resolute.

Anubis Correspondences:

Stone:	obsidian
Tree	yew
Feast	apple
Herb	savory
Flower	foxglove
Colour	black
Lucky number	3
Incense	kyphi
Animal	jackal
Symbol	🜨

Other symbols associated with Anubis: fetish, flail

Anubis Working

Light the candle and incense/oil, and compose yourself before your altar.

Close your eyes and breathe deeply for a couple of minutes, calming yourself, and casting off everyday thoughts and cares.

Visualisation

Imagine that you are walking in the great Necropolis at Giza at night. The moon is bright, casting long shadows. Here, the mighty pyramids dominate the scene, but there are many lesser tombs and graveyards throughout the complex. This is a time when the Necropolis was whole, some of it newly built, some of it already ancient. Its atmosphere is sombre, yet peaceful.

You reach the centre of a cemetery and here raise your arms to recite the invocation to Anubis.

"O Anubis, Mighty Anpu,
Jackal God of the Sacred Land
I call upon you.
Protect me from all ills that approach from the east.
O Anubis, Dweller in the Halls of Time,
Protect me from all ills that approach from the south.
Anpu, Guardian at the Gates of Dawn,
Protect me from all ills that approach from the west.
Api-Abu, Counter of Hearts,
Protect me from all ills that approach from the north.
Anpu, Power of the Light Within the Caves,
Remain at all times about me.
Khenti-seh-neter, Khenti-seh-neter.

Lord of the Sacred Land,
When I cannot hear, lead me.
Anpu, Light of the Two Worlds,
When I cannot see, show me the way.
O Anubis, He Whose Face is Golden as the Day,
Let me recognise and seize the opportunities that I am granted.
O Anubis, He Who is Upon His Mountain,
Let your hand work through me.
Guide me to my path of destiny.
Grant me now your power.
Khenti-seh-neter, Khenti-seh-neter."

(Egyptian Pronunciation: ken-*tee say* net-*er*
Meaning: god of the sacred land.)

You see an immense black dog walking through the shadows towards you. He is sleek like a greyhound, with long pointed ears and snout. This is Anubis in his jackal form. As he draws nearer, he transforms into a jackal-headed man. He wears a knee-length kilt of linen and embellished leather, and a wide decorative collar of beads that covers part of his chest. He carries an ankh and a flail. Anubis stands tall before you, awaiting your word.

If you are here to ask for his insight and to be shown the truth of a matter, visualise clearly all aspects of the situation and the outcome you wish to occur.

If you seek his protection as a guardian, either in the home or another location, again give Anubis clear images of what is required, and how you wish to be protected. Do not ask for Anubis to attack intruders or stalkers – he is simply to act as a deterrent, perhaps instilling fear and caution but not initiating violence. You could show him the layout of your home, or any other pertinent location, so he knows the route to guard it. Visualise him standing in the shadows of your home, alert for intruders. Imagine a strong energy emanating from him that will make wrong-doers think twice before approaching.

You can also create a phrase or short invocation to use whenever you are walking alone, or find yourself in some kind of threatening situation. By giving Anubis the 'code' for this, you may invoke his protective presence at any time or place.

Whatever you are petitioning for, make sure you visualise exactly how you want the end result to be, so that Anubis can see these images in your mind clearly. If appropriate, show everyone connected with the situation being content and unharmed by whatever occurs.

When you are finished, thank Anubis for his aid and see him depart.

Breathe slowly and deeply and imagine that your visualised surroundings fade away, to be replaced by your environment in the real world. When you are ready, open your eyes.

Anubis Attending the Dead
Tomb Painting

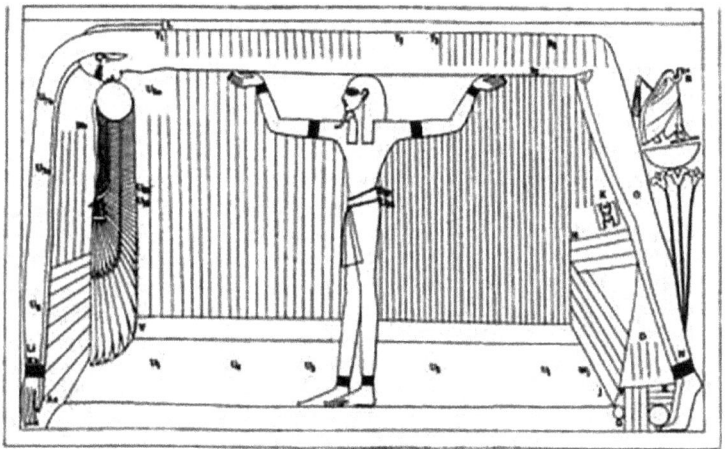

Shu Holding Up the Sky, Depicted as the Goddess Nut

Appendix

Natal Influences on Personality: Science or Superstition?

Graham Phillips

The zodiac signs are the twelve constellations, or patterns of stars, which fall in the band of sky through which the sun, moon and planets appear to move: Aries, Taurus, Gemini and so on. According to astrology, the positions of these heavenly bodies within the zodiac help shape our personalities and determine our destiny. Even today, in our complex, technological world, millions across the globe swear to the accuracy of their astrological birth sign, and just as many regularly consult their horoscopes in newspapers and magazines. Are they all deluded? Or does astrology really work?

In the late 20th century, a number of research projects were initiated to investigate astrology, many concluding that astrological birth charts prove far more accurate than should be expected by chance alone. Perhaps the most famous was the work of the French statistician – Françoise Gauquelin, who in the 1930s examined the horoscopes of thousands of sportsmen, actors and scientists, concluding that their achievements had been influenced by their date of birth. Although Gauquelin's findings were initially criticised by other researchers, many, including the renowned psychologist Hans Eysenck, finally endorsed his results.

Most scientists, however, remained – and still remain – firmly sceptical. Regardless of any statistical evidence that may support the case for astrology, the very idea that the stars can influence our daily lives seems completely contrary to the laws of physics. For most scientists, astrology continues to occupy the realms of magic and superstition.

But few astrologers consider themselves occultists or magicians. Some see their subject as an art, others as science, but most believe that one day some natural explanation will be found to account for why, in their opinion, astrology really works.

Before considering the evidence for or against astrology, it is important to understand something about the nature of the universe, how the cosmos was envisaged in the past, during the birth and development of astrology, and how it is understood today.

The Infinite Cosmos

In the 6th century BC, the Greek mathematician Pythagoras, challenged the widely-held theory that the earth was a huge flat disc floating on water. He claimed instead that it was a gigantic sphere. In a time centuries before the invention of space flight, how did he manage to get this right?

Pythagoras' reasoning concerned three observations: the disappearance of ships over the horizon, the shape the earth's shadow on the moon, and the appearance of new stars in the night sky when travelling north or south around the curvature of the earth. Pythagoras, and others who arrived at the same conclusion, however, still believed that the earth was the centre of the universe. To them, not only the moon, but also the sun and the planets, orbited the earth.

Three centuries after Pythagoras, Aristarchus of Samos, in the third century BC, announced that the earth moved around the sun. Unfortunately, unlike Pythagoras, he was not taken seriously. During the second century AD, the Egyptian geographer Ptolemy established the theory that became the accepted model of the universe for the next twelve centuries: the notion that the earth was fixed at the centre of the universe and everything else circled around it.

To both the ancient astronomer and astrologer alike, the universe was a vast hollow sphere on which the stars were fixed. Some believed that the stars were divine beings, while others saw them as distant windows, through which shone the light of heaven beyond. Called the firmament, this huge sphere was thought to rotate, with the stationary earth at its centre.

The stars of the firmament seemed to move around the earth, but remained in fixed positions relative to one another. Five bright, star-like objects, however, did not appear to be attached to the firmament. Instead, they seemed to wander at will over the backdrop of stars. They were called planets, from a Greek word meaning literally 'to wander'. There were five visible planets: Mercury, Venus, Mars, Jupiter and Saturn, which together with the sun and moon, (which also moved amongst the stars), were thought to lie between the earth and the firmament.

To some, the sun, moon and planets were the gods themselves. To others, they were great lights on seven transparent concentric spheres. Later, the Romans established the importance of the planets in daily life, naming after them the days of the week: such as Saturday was Saturn's day, Sunday was the sun's day, and Monday was the day of the moon.

The modern conception of the solar system did not emerge until the early sixteenth century, heralded by Nicolaus Copernicus (1473-1543). Born in Poland, Copernicus was the first to challenge seriously the long-standing theories of Ptolemy. Copernicus concluded that both the earth and the planets moved around the sun, and that the reason it appears the other way around is that the earth itself revolves once every twenty-four hours. Most astronomers refused to accept the Copernicus theory, and it was not until the time of Galileo, a century later, that his ideas were finally accepted.

Although Copernicus was wrong in his assumption that the

sun itself was the fixed central point of the universe, he identified that the movements of the heavenly bodies had been misunderstood. He established the difference between apparent and relative motions. In other words, from the viewpoint of someone standing on the rotating earth, the sun appears to be moving around the world and also slowly across the stars during the course of the year. In reality, the sun is not moving around the zodiac, the earth is moving slowly around the sun.

Once this principle was understood, it changed the astronomer's view of the universe. It was gradually accepted that the human race lived on a planet that was itself moving through space, and took a year to orbit the sun. The next question to be answered, however, was why this should happen at all. Why did the earth and the other planets continuously orbit the sun? The answer involved the principles of gravity, discovered by Isaac Newton in the late seventeenth century.

Newton's 'Law of Gravity' states that every object in the universe attracts every other object. The more massive the objects, or the closer together, the greater the attraction. Thus the earth exerts its greater gravitational force on a ball by making it fall to the ground if it is thrown.

This same principle applies to the earth itself, in that it is attracted to the greater mass of the sun. However, in this case, the momentum of the earth through space counteracts the sun's pull. In other words, when the planet formed, billions of years ago, the earth was too close to the sun to escape its gravity but was moving fast enough through space to prevent it from moving towards the sun. It is therefore forced to orbit the sun at approximately the same distance for ever, neither able to move towards nor pull away from the sun's attraction.

In order to chart the heavens, astronomers required more than just the twelve signs of the zodiac to distinguish one part of the sky from another. There are in fact eighty-eight constellations, constructed from patterns of the brightest visible stars. The constellations lend their names to the eighty-eight areas into which the sky is divided for the purposes of identifying and charting celestial objects. Any heavenly body – stars, galaxies, comets, asteroids, planets – fall somewhere within this constellation sky map. With so many constellations, it might seem puzzling that the sun, moon and all the planets only appear to move within the band of the twelve signs of the zodiac. The reason is that the planets are all on virtually the same orbital plane around the sun. The moon – although orbiting the earth – moves through roughly the same plane. In astronomical terms, this plane is called the ecliptic, and the zodiac covers a zone some 8.5 degrees to either side.

One of the main reasons that Copernicus' rotating earth theory was not believed was that it failed to account for the fact that the zodiac itself moved up and down in the course of the year. Copernicus claimed that the firmament, the backdrop of stars, occupied a fixed position in space, although it appeared to revolve because the earth itself was rotating. His opponents argued that even if this was true, the firmament still moved; during summer it tilted in one direction and during the winter it tilted in the other. The true reason for this apparent motion of the stars is that the earth's axis is tilted towards the sun at an angle of 23.5 degrees.

The ancient astronomers were accurate in one respect; the moon does orbit the earth. The moon is much smaller than the earth. It orbits the earth once every twenty-seven days. This may seem strange, considering that there is a new moon approximately every twenty-nine and a half days. The reason for this is that the earth itself is orbiting the sun. In the twenty-seven days it takes for the moon to go around the earth, the earth moves further along in its orbit around the sun. It takes about two and a half days for the moon to catch up and be back in line with the sun.

Earth is not the only planet to have moons. Mars has two and Jupiter has twelve, while Mercury and Venus have none. One thing that the planets do have in common is that they are all in orbit around the sun; collectively called the solar system. Essentially, the sun is a gigantic mass of compressed gases, continuously-burning in an ongoing series of nuclear reactions. The heart of the solar system, the sun is orbited by the planets and their moons, thousands of asteroids and hundreds of icy comets. As far as we know there are nine planets. Nearest to the sun is Mercury, followed by Venus and then the earth, Further out comes Mars, Jupiter and Saturn. All these are visible with the naked eye and were known to the ancients. In recent centuries, three further planets have been discovered in the outer reaches of the solar system: Uranus, discovered in 1781, Neptune in 1846 and Pluto in 1930.

The Romans thought that the planets were gods and their names are still used today.

The Evidence for Astrology

Today's understanding of the enormity and complexity of the universe is very different from the conceptions held by ancient astronomers. To the Greeks, Romans and other archaic civilisations, who founded the principles of astrology, the firmament of stars was only just out of reach, while the sun, moon and planets were the gods overseeing human destiny.

From a scientific standpoint, the stars and planets are simply too far away to have any direct effect upon the daily life of Earth's inhabitants. Astrologers may argue that there are other forces at work, which science has not yet recognised. However, few scientists are prepared to speculate about something for which, in their opinion, there is no evidence.

In recent years, the case for astrology, (at least certain aspects of it), has been considerably strengthened. There may be, after all, measurable cosmic forces influencing human characteristics, personality and behaviour.

Although the stars may be too distant to affect our daily existence, the same is not true of the sun and moon. Apart from providing us with the heat and light necessary for survival, the sun, (or at least the earth's angle to it), determines the seasons.

The moon, on the other hand, exerts direct gravitational influence over the ocean tides. Moreover, the moon has long been associated with the human condition: its month closely corresponds to the female menstrual cycle, and its apparent effect on human behaviour resulted in the unfortunate word 'lunatic' being coined for people suffering certain types of mental illness. Renowned scientists in the 20th century discovered previously unsuspected solar and lunar influences on the human body.

Japan's Maki Takata examined the influence of sunspot activity on blood pressure, discovering a close relationship between the two. Italy's Georgio Piccardi showed that both sunspots and the monthly cycle of the moon affect various chemical reactions in the body. And America's David Levinson demonstrated that both men and women have a delicate sensitivity to the moon's gravitational field. But perhaps most astonishing, regarding astrology, was the work of the British research team led by Dr Lewis Atkinson in 1985.

Atkinson's research indicated that the moon's gravity directly influenced the development of tiny organisms. Although the effect in fully-grown and complex life forms, such as humans, is minimal, it may well be sufficient to influence an embryo.

Although personality is shaped by environment, genetics moulds our basic character – our inbuilt starting point. That is why two young children may respond very differently to the same conditions; one clinging to an overbearing parent, another rebelling. Genetically inherited, these characteristics may be modified in the early development of the foetus by the gravitational influence of the moon.

To understand how the moon might affect genetic attributes, we must first appreciate that a living organism is a complex arrangement of self-replicating molecules. Simply described, the atoms that make up matter are comprised of a nucleus around which electrons move. When atoms exist in groups, bonded together, they are called molecules, and a substance comprised of only one type of atom is called an element. When atoms of different elements combine, they form the molecules of a compound, with the properties often remarkably different from the original elements from which they were composed. For example, an atom of the soft metal sodium, which reacts explosively with water, and an atom of the poisonous gas chlorine combine to form a molecule of edible common salt. The properties and behaviour of a substance often depends more on the shape of its molecules than on the atoms from which it is formed. It is in the tiny microcosm that the lunar effects on organisms occur.

A molecule known as deoxyribonucleic acid is responsible for life as we know it. Deoxyribonucleic acid, or DNA, has the unique ability to reproduce itself. It is the essence of life itself, for without DNA the cells that form a living organism could not divide and grow.

DNA is concentrated in the nucleus of each cell, containing instructions as to what the cell should become. Some cells develop more efficient ways of breaking down food and become stomach cells, some acquire a hard membrane and become skin, while others become sensitive to light and form eyes. Incredibly, the nucleus of a fertilised egg contains all the instructions for the development of a fully-grown creature. Called the genetic code, it determines everything from the colour of hair to the size of the nose.

The DNA at the heart of the cell can be thought of as a miniature computer programme, although infinitely more complex. We know that some external factors can damage or modify this program, such as chemical effects or radiation, which in extreme cases may result in deformity or mutation. Another influencing factor, demonstrated by the Atkinson research, is the gravitational pull of the moon.

The Atkinson findings suggested that the moon's gravity affects the internal cell structure by causing slight variations in the build-up of nucleotides – the building blocks of DNA –

during each twenty-nine and a half day month of the moon. During a new moon, when the sun and moon are exerting a gravitational pull from the same direction, the influence is different from the time of a full moon, when the gravitational influence of the two bodies are from opposite directions. In a multi-cellular organism, this has no noticeable influence, as the genetic program is already established. However, in the single cell of a fertilised egg, the genetic coding can be subtly modified. Consequently, mental and physiological characteristics might well be modified by the moon at the time of conception or during foetal development.

There was also another interesting point in the Atkinson findings. The lunar effect varied, depending on the time of year. Put simply, the lunar effect ran in roughly 28-day months, which gradually altered as the year progressed. Although the moon months may influence our eventual characteristics, how might the changing seasons be involved?

Modern scientific studies have been made regarding the seasonal effects of sunlight upon the annual biological rhythms of organisms. The growth patterns of plants, such as blossom in spring, fruit in summer and leaf-fall in autumn, are completely synchronised with the seasons. Animals also experience seasonal alterations: hibernation in winter, breeding in spring, and migration in autumn, are just a few of the ways in which the animal kingdom responds to the seasons. These annual changes are due almost exclusively to the availability of sunlight; the organism responds to the lengthening and shortening of daylight. For example, following summer, around mid-September, when day and night are of equal duration, the tree is stimulated to start losing its leaves, while the squirrel prepares for hibernation. After winter, when day and night are again of equal duration around mid-March, the tree's leaves begin to grow and the squirrel awakes.

There can be little doubt that the length of daylight is the stimulus responsible for these changes. If a creature from the northern hemisphere is taken to the southern hemisphere, before long its behaviour patterns adapt; the same is true for the growth of plants. The relocated animal does not hibernate in the height of summer, and tree's leaves do not fall in the spring.

Modern studies have discovered many variations in human bodily and mental activity, which correspond to seasonal change. In the wild, an alteration of behaviour and metabolism was essential for our ancestors' survival. The gathering and hoarding instinct was imperative during summer months, so that early humans would prepare for winter. Less activity was equally essential in winter, when energy needed to be conserved.

In most of us, the seasonal response mechanisms are not overtly apparent. However, even in our technological world, where daily life continues to a large degree unaltered by summer or winter, a considerable number of people still respond to winter in an almost disabling manner.

In 1984, psychiatrists at the National Institute of Mental Health in Maryland, USA, were among the first to identify a syndrome known as the Seasonal Affected Disorder, or SAD for short. In autumn, shortly after the days become shorter than the nights, sufferers from SAD begin to feel their energy declining. They oversleep and have difficulty rising in the morning. However, even though they are sleeping more, they still feel exceedingly tired during the day. Furthermore, they eat too much, especially carbohydrates, and their weight increases. Eventually, they become lethargic, and have difficulty thinking, processing information, or carrying on with their work. Sometimes, the problem can become so severe that they completely withdraw from social activities, and may even be unable to hold down a job. In extreme cases, the syndrome is virtually incapacitating. Paradoxically, those with SAD are experiencing a condition that would have been immensely beneficial to their remote ancestors.

For years, psychiatrists and physicians failed to recognise

the seasonal pattern of SAD, and traditional therapy and drug treatment had little or no benefit. It is now known that, like creatures in the wild, SAD sufferers respond to the availability of daylight. Today, the condition is treated by tricking the patient's physiology into believing that it is summer all year round. Standard artificial lighting is not sufficiently bright to simulate daylight, but by exposing the patient to high-luminosity fluorescent lights for two hours every morning, SAD is alleviated in nearly all sufferers. Exposure to light that mimics the intensity of sunlight just after dawn – light therapy, as it is called – makes the patient's sunlight responsive system believe that the days are longer than they actually are. With light therapy, the patient quickly returns to summertime alertness.

These seasonal responses to sunlight, and other yearly changes, are known as circannual rhythms, and are responsible for many other subtle variations in bodily activity, including hormonal balance. Although detailed study is still in its early stages, it is known that a human foetus is modified by the circannual rhythms of its mother. Infants who undergo specific stages of embryonic development at the same time of year may therefore share characteristic behavioural and physiological traits. In other words, someone conceived in December, for example, will be affected differently to someone conceived in June. The eventual date of birth may therefore be an important factor in determining various aspects of the child's psychology and physiology. As pregnancy is nine months duration for almost every human being, most of us will have undergone foetal development during the same seasons as another who shares our birthday.

Circannual physiological alteration and behavioural change may account for the apparent accuracy of astrology. The date of birth may help determine human characteristics and also be responsible for certain aspects of behaviour at different times of the year. Someone born in Aries, for instance, would have undergone foetal development during the same seasonal period as another born in the same sign, and consequently would have experienced similar embryonic modifications. Someone born in Taurus, on the other hand, would have experienced slightly different modifications, shared by other Taureans. Not only might they be similar in personality, they are also likely to behave in a similar manner at the same times of year. This may explain how astrology could predict that during the sign of Capricorn, in the middle of winter, a Virgo may do one thing and a Gemini another.

In modern astrology, the exact time and place of birth is needed to compile what many believe to be an accurate horoscope. The precise positions of the sun, moon and planets are then plotted and their relative positions in the zodiac are interpreted. The popular horoscope, however, concerns solely the sun's position in the zodiac, and so, it is argued, is only broadly applicable. Consequently, the apparent accuracy of modern sun-sign astrology in predicting general human characteristics and behaviour may well be the result of circannual rhythms.

These latest scientific discoveries are of particular relevance to the system in this book – natal analysis based upon the months of the year. Unlike the familiar astrological zodiac, the character analyses using the Dendera system do not incorporate the positions of the stars and planets, but the phases of the moon and the seasons of the year. They incorporate the seasonal and lunar influences – both of which are now being shown to subtly influence human characteristics. It therefore seems quite within the realms of scientific feasibility that the Dendera zodiac – created thousands of years ago – might really offer a means of predicting human behaviour.

More Egyptian-Themed Magic
From Megalithica Books
immanion-press.com

Sekhem Heka by Storm Constantine

Drawing upon her experiences in Egyptian Magic and the energy healing systems of Reiki and Seichim, Storm Constantine developed this new system to appeal to practitioners of both magic and energy healing. Incorporating ritual and visualisation into a progressive journey through the seven energy centres of the body, Sekhem Heka can be practiced by those who are already attuned to an energy healing modality, as well as those who are simply interested in the magical aspects of the system. Sekhem Heka is designed to help the practitioner work upon self-evolution and self-knowledge. Each of the seven tiers focuses upon a particular Ancient Egyptian god or goddess, including practical exercises and rites.
ISBN pbk: 9781905713134, $21.99, £12.99

Graeco-Egyptian Magic by Tony Mierzwicki

Graeco-Egyptian Magick outlines a daily practice involving planetary Hermeticism, drawn from original texts and converted into a format that fits easily into the modern magician's practice. Graeco-Egyptian magick represents the last flowering of paganism before it was wiped out by Christianity. It blends ancient Sumerian and Egyptian magick with the relatively more modern Greek and Judaic systems. It includes a recreation of a planetary system of self-initiation using authentic Graeco-Egyptian practices from the first five centuries C.E. This is a practical intermediate level text aimed at those who are serious about their spiritual development and already have grounding in basic spirituality, but beginners who carefully follow the instructions sequentially should not be deterred. ISBN pbk: 1905713037, $21.99, £12.99

The Travellers' Guide to the Duat by Kiya Nicoll

Planning a trip to the Egyptian spirit world? Like any responsible traveller, you want to know something about the history, geography, and politics of your destination. You want to know what documents you need to have in order for customs and immigration, what precautions to take, how to book a boat tour, where to stay, what to eat, and when you'll get the most interesting sightseeing opportunities. Laced through its humorous presentation you will find extensive information about ancient Egyptian religion and magical practice. Renditions of ancient spells in modern poetry mark each section, showing the ancient magical texts in a new light. The Beautiful West awaits! Book your tour today!
ISBN pbk: 9781905713738, $19.99, £10.99

Recent Titles from Megalithica Books

Coming Forth by Day by Storm Constantine

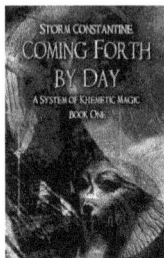

This book explores the myths of Ancient Egyptian gods and goddesses – showing how their stories relate to aspects of our lives, hopes and aspirations, and how we can learn from these ancient narratives. Through 28 deep and evocative pathworkings and rituals, the author provides a rich and vivid system of magic that the practitioner – whether experienced or a novice – can utilise in the search for self-knowledge, and to help themselves, others and the world around them. ISBN: 978-1-912241-11-8 Price: £12.99, $16.99

SHE: Primal Meetings with the Dark Goddess by Storm Constantine & Andrew Collins

The Dark Goddess is unpredictable, dispassionate, cruel, and often deadly. She reflects our deepest desires, fears, hopes and expectations. In this fully-illustrated book, Storm Constantine and Andrew Collins have selected a fascinating range of 34 goddesses, including some who are not so well-known. The pathworkings to meet them and explore their realms will offer insight into these often-misunderstood deities. (This title is also available as a limited edition, numbered hardback.) ISBN: 978-1-912241-06-4 Price: £12.99, $18.99

My First Book of Magic by Dolores Ashcroft-Nowicki

I want to tell you how the Pagan Way works, what it does, and how it makes you feel. I want you to know the joy this oldest of all traditions can bring you. The way of sharing it with humans, elementals, sprites, animals, plants, trees, and of course other pagans.
If you have a child in your life that has the look of far memory in their eyes, gift them with this guide. If you remember the child you were, read this book and reopen the gates of your wonder." – Ivo Dominguez Jr., author of 'Keys to Perception'.
ISBN: 978-1-912241-10-1 Price: £10.99, $15.99

immanion-press.com

www.ingramcontent.com/pod-product-compliance
Lightning Source LLC
Chambersburg PA
CBHW031128090426
42738CB00008B/1005